1,001 PEARLS OF GOLFERS' WISDOM

1,001 PEARLS OF GOLFERS' WISDOM

Advice and Knowledge, from Tee to Green

JIM APFELBAUM
FOREWORD BY ARNOLD PALMER

Skyhorse Publishing

Skyhorse Publishing books may be purchased in bulk at special discounts for sales promotion, corporate gifts, fund-raising, or educational purposes. Special editions can also be created to specifications. For details, contact the Special Sales Department, Skyhorse Publishing, 307 West 36th Street, 11th Floor, New York, NY 10018 or info@skyhorsepublishing.com.

Skyhorse® and Skyhorse Publishing® are registered trademarks of Skyhorse Publishing, Inc.®, a Delaware corporation.

Visit our website at www.skyhorsepublishing.com.

10 9 8 7 6 5 4 3 2 1

Library of Congress Cataloging-in-Publication Data is available on file.

ISBN: 978-1-61608-354-0

Printed in China

Table of Contents

FOREWORD

Golf is my life, and I have been around the game for as long as I can remember. I was three years old when I first started hitting balls, and I spent a lot of time around the sport as a young boy, mostly because my father was the head professional and greens keeper at the Latrobe Country Club in Pennsylvania. I'd ride in his lap while he was mowing the fairways with his tractor and eat lunch with him under the shade trees that grew on the course. Years later, when I was 12, I entered my first junior golf tournament and went on to play on the Latrobe High School team. Then, I was off to Wake Forest, at which point I had won a few amateur tournaments

and started playing more on a national level.
By the time I turned professional in 1955, I had
won more than my fair share of titles, among
them the Ohio Amateur, and best of all, the
U.S. Amateur. And during my stints on both the
regular and senior PGA Tours in the years to
follow, I finished first in 73 events and added
another 19 titles in non-sanctioned tournaments
at home and abroad.

But for me golf was not only about playing in
tournaments. I've always enjoyed a simple
afternoon round with friends, and to this day, I love
any excuse to play. In fact, it sometimes feels as if
I have played every day of my adult life. And truth
be told, that is not so far off.

All of this is to say that I have been around the game for a very long time. And being around golf so much, I have been lucky to have seen amazing places and witnessed extraordinary things, whether walking the fairways or Augusta National, say, or the streets of St. Andrews. I have also heard more than my share of thoughts and comments on the sport, both on the course and at the 19th hole afterwards, and the hilarity of those words as well as the depth of their meaning are what prompted me to write this Foreword. For golf is often as much about the interaction with your friends as it is the shots we are playing, and enjoying the way players are able to laugh at themselves as they chuckle at—and with—others. It is also about reading accounts of what happens to other people when they tee it up, whether for fun or in competition, and the things that come out of their mouths. Because we, as golfers, say the darndest things.

There is so much in this volume that will make you laugh, starting with comments from comedic geniuses like Bill Murray, Bob Hope, and David Feherty and moving to longtime journalistic observers of the game, such as Grantland Rice, Peter Dobereiner, and the fellow who wrote my biography a few years ago, Jim Dodson. The words of Buddy Hackett and Leslie Nielsen have understandably found their way into this book, and even men and women who are not noted for their wit and humor can bring down the house when the subject is golf. For example, Hank

Aaron is not exactly a star at stand-up. But he can induce more than a few giggles when he says things like: "It took me 17 years to get 3,000 hits in baseball. I did that in one afternoon on the golf course."

But this publication of quotes is not only about laughs. It is also about insight into the game, from men like Ben Hogan and Bobby Jones who knew it intimately. It provides deeper takes on life itself, from the likes of Winston Churchill, President George H.W. Bush, and John D. Rockefeller. It even has a few lines from yours truly, as well as pearls of wisdom and wit from a few of my old competitors, like Jack Nicklaus and Gary Player as well as Billy Casper and Chi-Chi Rodriguez.

Culled from a variety of sources and edited by Jim Apfelbaum, they are sure to delight fans of the game for years to come.

I hope you enjoy it as much as I have.

—Arnold Palmer

CHAPTER 1

WHAT IS GOLF?: DEFINITIONS

Golf is life. If you can't take golf, you can't take life.

—Anonymous

Golf is a game whose aim it is to hit a very small ball into an even smaller hole, with weapons singularly ill-designed for the purpose.

—Winston Churchill

Golf is the cruelest of sports. Like life, it's unfair. It's a harlot. A trollop. It leads you on. It never lives up to its promises . . . It's a boulevard of broken dreams. It plays with men. And runs off with the butcher.

—Jim Murray

Golf is an open exhibition of overweening ambition, courage deflated by stupidity, skill soured by a whiff of arrogance.

—Alistair Cooke

Golf is a funny game. It's done much for health and at the same time has ruined people by robbing them of their peace of mind. Look at me, I'm the healthiest idiot in the world.

—Bob Hope

Golf is the only game in which a precise knowledge of the rules can earn one a reputation for bad sportsmanship.

—Patrick Campbell

Golf is like life in a lot of ways: The most important competition is the one against yourself. All the biggest wounds are self-inflicted. And you get a lot of breaks you don't deserve, both ways. So it's important not to get too upset when you're having a bad day.

—Bill Clinton

Golf is not a funeral, though both can be very sad affairs.

—Bernard Darwin

They say that life is a lot like golf—don't believe them. Golf is a lot more complicated.

—Gardner Dickinson

They call it golf because all of the other four-letter words were taken.

—Raymond Floyd

Golf is wonderful exercise. You can stand on your feet for hours, watching somebody else putt.

—Will Rogers

Golf is the only game where the worst player gets the best of it. He gets more out of it with regard to both exercise and enjoyment. The good player worries over the slightest mistake, whereas the poor player makes too many mistakes to worry over them.

—David Lloyd George, British PM

Golf is a game that needlessly prolongs the lives of some of our most useless citizens.
—Bob Hope

Happiness is a long walk with a putter in your hand.
—Wayne Grady

A good one iron shot is about as easy to come by as an understanding wife.
—Dan Jenkins

Golf is more fun than walking naked in a strange place, but not much.
—Buddy Hackett

Golf is an ineffectual attempt to put an elusive ball into an obscure hole with implements ill-adapted to the purpose.

—Woodrow Wilson

Playing golf is like raising children: You keep thinking you'll do better next time.

—Roy McKie

Local rules in golf: a set of regulations that are ignored by players on a specific course rather than by golfers as a whole.

—E.C. McKenzie

Golf is like any other sports competition. There is not a whole lot of point to it unless someone suffers.

—Kevin Wohl

Golf is the Esperanto of sport. All over the world, golfers talk the same language—much of it nonsense and much unprintable—endure the same frustrations, discover the same infallible secrets of putting, share the same illusory joys.

—Henry Longhurst

This is just a game. That's all it is. It's not a war.

—Jack Nicklaus

Golf is a game not just of manners but of morals.

—Art Spander

Great southpaw golfers are more scarce than a clear day in Los Angeles.

—Joe Schwendeman

Golf keeps the heart young and the eyes clear.

—Andrew Kirkaldy

Golf is like faith: it is the substance of things hoped for, the evidence of things not seen.

—Arnold Haultain

Golf is a game of expletives not deleted.
—Dr. Irving A. Gladstone

Golf is a good walk spoiled.
—Mark Twain

Professional golf is the only sport where, if you win twenty percent of the time, you're the best.
—Jack Nicklaus

Golf and women are a lot alike. You know you are not going to wind up with anything but grief, but you can't resist the impulse.
—Jackie Gleason

Golf is a fine relief from the tensions of office, but we are a little tired of holding the bag.

—Adlai Stevenson, on Eisenhower's love of golf

Golf is essentially an exercise in masochism conducted out-of-doors.

—Paul O'Neil

Golf is very much like a love affair: if you don't take it seriously, it's no fun; if you do, it breaks your heart. Don't break your heart, but flirt with the possibility.

—Louise Suggs

Golf combines two favorite American pastimes: taking long walks and hitting things with a stick.

—P.J. O'Rourke

Golf is a lot like sex. Even when you cheat you still have to get it up and in. And that gets tougher and tougher to do every year.

—Billy Orvile

Putting is like wisdom—partly a natural gift and partly the accumulation of experience.

—Arnold Palmer

Golf is a game in which you claim the privileges of age and retain the playthings of childhood.

> —Samuel Johnson

Golf is the pursuit of the infinite.

> —Jim Murray

Golf is good for the soul.

> —Will Rogers

The difference between golf and the government is that in golf you can't improve your lie.

> —George Deukmejian

Golf is a game kings and presidents play when they get tired of running countries.

—Charles Price

Golf is a lot like sex. It's something you can enjoy all your life. And if you remain an amateur, you get to pick your own playing partners.

—Jess Sweetser

Golf is like chasing a quinine pill around a cow pasture.

—Winston Churchill

Hockey is a sport for white men. Basketball is a sport for black men. Golf is a sport for white men dressed like black pimps.

—Tiger Woods

The golf swing is like a suitcase into which we are trying to pack one too many things.

—John Updike

Golf is like acting in that both require concentration and relaxation at the same time.

—Jane Seymour

Golf is like solitaire. When you cheat, you cheat only yourself.

—Tony Lema

21

If you watch a game, it's fun. If you play at it, it's recreation. If you work at it, it's golf.

—Bob Hope

Golf is a day spent in a round of strenuous idleness.

—William Wordsworth

The perfect game of golf has never been played. It's 18 holes in one.

—Ben Hogan

In golf, humiliations are the essence of the game.

—Alistair Cooke

Golf is typical capitalist lunacy.
                    —George Bernard Shaw

Golf is, in part, a game, but only in part. It
is also part of a religion, a fervor, a vice,
a mirage, a frenzy, a fear, an abscess, a
joy, a thrill, a pest, a disease, an uplift, a
brooding melancholy, a dream of yesterday, a
disappointing today, and a hope for tomorrow.
                    —Grantland Rice

Don Quixote would understand golf. It is the
impossible dream.
                    —Jim Murray

Golf is the indispensable adjunct of high civilization.

—Andrew Carnegie

Golf is a game for people who are not active enough for baseball.

—William Howard Taft

Golf is a game in which you yell 'fore,' shoot six, and write down five.

—Paul Harvey

Too dull. It's a visual-neurological sport. It's so ridiculous.

—Ralph Nader

Golf, especially championship golf, isn't
supposed to be fun, was never meant to be
fair, and never will make any sense.

—Charles Price

Golf remains, now as always, a sport geared
toward fat men in plaid pants who think that
Fortune magazine is racy.

—Joe Queenan

CHAPTER 2

COMPETITION—ON WINNING, LOSING, AND THE PURSUIT OF EXCELLENCE

Winning isn't everything, but wanting it is.

—Arnold Palmer

No one remembers who came in second.

—Walter Hagen

I think the biggest pressure comes from myself, I have very high expectations . . . I always feel like when I come to a tournament I want to be ready to play and that's one of the reasons I don't play as many events. I want my game to be top notch and I want every chance to win.

—Annika Sörenstam

I was criticized for many years for being unsociable, but for me, how can you be mates with people you're trying to beat?

—Nick Faldo

I know there's a lot of guys who would love to see me fail. Well, good. Let 'em. I'm glad.

—John Daly

Hell, it ain't like losing a leg!

—Billy Joe Patton, on losing the Masters

Good golfing temperament falls between taking it with a grin or shrug and throwing a fit.

—Sam Snead

It's wonderful how you can start with three strangers in the morning, play 18 holes and by the time the day is over you have three solid enemies.

—Bob Hope

The average golfer doesn't play golf. He attacks it.

—Jack Burke Jr.

Only way you beat Ben is if God wanted you to.

—Tommy Bolt, on Ben Hogan

In those days, the money was the main thing, the only thing I played for. Titles were something to grow old with.

—Byron Nelson,
on playing to win in the 1937 Masters

If I ever get bored with golf, I'm going to start over and play left-handed.

—Michelle Wie

Competitive golf has been the center of both our lives, and yet the differences between us—the actors that made us such intense and faithful competitors, I believe—are still as apparent to anyone who wishes to take time to look.

—Arnold Palmer, on Jack Nicklaus,
from *A Golfer's Life* with James Dodson

To succeed at anything, you must have a huge ego. I'm not talking about confidence. Confidence is self-assurance for a reason. Ego is self-assurance for no good reason.

—Frank Beard

Yeah. I think when I play golf, yes, I think I have to make the world revolve around me. If you want to be the best at something, you have to make it revolve around what you are doing. Is that clear?

—Jack Nicklaus, *Golf Digest*

The truly great things happen when a genius is alone. This is true especially among golfers.

—J.R. Coulson

When I'm in contention coming down to those last few holes . . . it is a miserable, sick, lonely feeling. You're so scared, sometimes you can't see. But when I can pull off a good shot on those holes, that's what I look forward to. And I figure I haven't won nearly enough.

—Sandra Palmer (winner of 21 LPGA events)

I'm a perfectionist. I have to win. If I can't be best at anything I try I'd just quit.

—Beth Daniel

Miss this little putt for fifteen hundred? I should say not.

—Walter Hagen, before sinking a 10-footer

The kids on the Tour today are too good at losing. Show me a 'good loser' and I'll show you a 'seldom winner.'

—Sam Snead

The mark of a great player is in his ability to come back. The great champions have all come back from defeat.

—Sam Snead

It's nice to have the opportunity to play for so much money, but it's nicer to win it.

—Patty Sheehan

You're a good loser if you can grip the winner's hand without wishing it was his throat.

—Hal Chadwick

I'm here because golf is my sport and I like to compete . . . Just by being here I'm already beginning to win.

—Seve Ballesteros

Never let up. The more you can win by, the more doubts you put in the other players' minds the next time out.

—Sam Snead

I dreamed I made 17 holes in one, and then on the 18th hole I lipped the cup and I was madder than hell.

—Ben Hogan

Having a good time is winning the tournament.

—Jan Stephenson

How can they beat me? I've been struck by lightning, had two back operations, and been divorced twice.

—Lee Trevino

There is a constant truth about tournament golf. Other men have to lose a championship before one man can win it.

—Dan Jenkins

He didn't beat me, sir. I beat myself, I beat myself.

—J.H. Taylor

Most golfers prepare for disaster. A good golfer prepares for success.

—Bob Toski

More matches are lost through carelessness at the beginning than any other cause.

—Harry Vardon

You haven't got a chance . . . I mean, I own the place!

—Donald Trump

I'm going to win so much money this year, my caddie will make the top twenty money winner's list.

—Lee Trevino

Thank you. How did you do?

—Ben Hogan, to Clayton Heafner,
who finished second at the 1951 US Open,
two strokes behind Hogan

Victory is everything. You can spend the money, but you can never spend the memories.

—Ken Venturi

Golf is a game of days, and I can beat anyone on my day.

—Fuzzy Zoeller

I think I fail a bit less than everyone else.

—Jack Nicklaus

I learned how to win by losing and not liking it.

—Tom Watson

It's not whether you win or lose—but whether I win or lose.

—Sandy Lyle

If your adversary is badly bunkered, there is no rule against your standing over him and counting his strokes aloud, with increasing gusto as their number mounts up; but it will be a wise precaution to arm yourself with the niblick before doing so, so as to meet him on equal terms.

—Horace Hutchinson

I'm tired of giving it my best and not having it be good enough.

—Jack Nicklaus

I see no reason why a golf course cannot be played in 18 birdies. Just because no one has ever done that doesn't mean it can't be done.
—Ben Hogan

My game was my business and as a business it demanded constant playing in the championship bracket, for a current title was my selling commodity.
—Walter Hagen, from *The Walter Hagen Story*

But then there's a little part of me that says, 'You know what? I still think I can get better, I still think I can do this and that.' That's what keeps me going.
—Annika Sörenstam

If money titles meant anything, I'd play more tournaments. The only thing that means a lot to me is winning. If I have more wins than anybody else and win more majors than anybody else in the same year, then it's been a good year.

—Tiger Woods

I'm happy out of my mind. I like beating a lot of people.

—Michelle Wie

I'm trying as hard as I can, and sometimes things don't go your way, and that's the way things go.

—Tiger Woods

Every golfer has a little monster in him. It's just that type of sport.

—Fuzzy Zoeller

Every time I'd get close to a major prize, my hands would begin to shake, and for a moment or two, when it counted most, the demons of doubt would whisper in my ear and I honestly wondered if I could win again.

—Arnold Palmer, on the decline of his game

I beat Tiger Woods by five strokes—but he was only six at the time.

—Gregg Zaun

Here is a philosophy of boldness to take
advantage of every tiny opening toward victory.
—Arnold Palmer

No, I don't go places for sentiment—I have
that at home. I came here believing I had a
chance . . . to win.
—Ben Hogan, asked at age 53 if he came to
the Masters for sentimental reasons

I'd like to thank Tom and Ed for missing all
those putts.
—Fuzzy Zoeller, after winning the 1979
Masters

I'm the best. I just haven't played yet.
—Muhammad Ali

Who's going to be second?

> —Walter Hagen, before a tournament

I play with friends, but we don't play friendly games.

> —Ben Hogan

Be brave if you lose and meek if you win.

> —Harvey Penick

You hear that winning breeds winning. But no winners are bred from losing. They learn that they don't like it.

> —Tom Watson

I like trying to win. That's what golf is all about.
—Jack Nicklaus

I look into their eyes, shake their hand, pat their back, and wish them luck, but I am thinking, 'I am going to bury you.'
—Seve Ballesteros

I can tell right away if a guy is a winner or a loser just by the way he conducts himself on the course.
—Donald Trump

Over the first three rounds you're playing the course. In the final round, if you're in contention, you're playing the man.

—Jack Nicklaus

I've always made a total effort, even when the odds seemed entirely against me. I never quit trying; I never felt that I didn't have a chance to win.

—Arnold Palmer

When talents are equal, it's the extra effort
that makes the difference in the close ones.
In almost every endeavor, success or failure
depends on execution, precision, inches,
seconds, unbelievable skill, unbelievable
performances, unbelievable happenings.

—Jack Whitaker

The sweetest two words are 'next time.' The
sourest word is 'if.'

—Chi-Chi Rodriguez

Forget your opponents; always play against par.

—Sam Snead

I never knew what top golf was like until I turned professional. Then it was too late.

—Steve Melnyk

He comes onto a tee looking like a prize fighter climbing into the ring ready for a world championship bout.

—Charles Price, on Arnold Palmer

CHAPTER 3

MENTAL GAME—
MOTIVATION, RISK,
CONTROL, AND LUCK

Ninety percent of golf is played from the
shoulders up.

—Deacon Palmer

The mark of a champion is the ability to make
the most of good luck and the best of bad.

—Anonymous

The only shots you can be sure of are those
you've had already.

—Byron Nelson

This game is so elusive. You try to maintain the
peaks and level up the valleys.

—Tom Watson

In golf you almost always beat yourself or are destroyed by the game.

—Al Barkow

In golf, as in no other sport, your principal opponent is yourself.

—Herbert Warren Wind

The mind messes up more shots than the body.

—Tommy Bolt

Of the mental hazards, being scared is the worst.

—Sam Snead

There's a heightened sense of pressure on every shot, and there's no sense denying it. Recognize it, and deal with it.

—Mike Weir

When I play my best golf, I feel as if I'm in a fog, standing back watching the earth in orbit with a golf club in my hands.

—Mickey Wright

Golf puts a man's character on the anvil and his richest qualities—patience, poise, restraint—to the flame.

—Billy Casper

The word is control. That's my ultimate—to have control.

—Nick Faldo

Success depends almost entirely on how effectively you learn to manage the game's two ultimate adversaries: the course and yourself.

—Jack Nicklaus

Through the ball we are all the same. We just have different ways of getting there.

—Charles Coody

These guys have no fear? Not to them, it's not; they've been doing it all their lives.

—Butch Harmon

To play well you must feel tranquil and at peace. I have never been troubled by nerves in golf because I felt I had nothing to lose and everything to gain.

—Harry Vardon

It's funny . . . you need a fantastic memory in this game to remember the great shots and a very short memory to forget the bad ones.

—Gary McCord

If you're stupid enough to whiff, you should be smart enough to forget it.

—Arnold Palmer

Once the golfing champion allows himself to suspect that playing a superb round is not the be-all and end-all of life he is lost.

—Anonymous

Listen to your heart and your gut. That small voice inside you. How often have you left the house knowing you've forgotten something, and it turns out you have? Intuition is very powerful, and certainly it's true in golf.

—Nick Faldo

My ability to concentrate and work toward that goal has been my greatest asset.

—Jack Nicklaus

If you expect a bad lie for even one second, the gods will know it and give you a bad lie.

—Michelle Wie

I'm not really interested in sports psychology. It makes me feel like a crazy person.

—Michelle Wie

A few disasters resulting from a desire to display brilliant technique are enough to harden even the most sensitive nature . . . Once the round is under way, the business at hand becomes that of getting results. Nothing else matters.

—Bobby Jones

However unlucky you may be, it really is not fair to expect your adversary's grief for your undeserved misfortunes to be as poignant as your own.

—Horace Hutchinson

I say this without any reservations whatsoever: It is impossible to outplay an opponent you can't outthink.

—Lawson Little

I do not remember any other golfer who did not consider himself, on the whole, a remarkably unlucky one.

—Sir Walter Simpson

My luck is so bad that if I bought a cemetery, people would stop dying.

—Ed Furgol

On the golf course, a man may be the dogged victim of inexorable fate, be struck down by an appalling stroke or tragedy, become the hero of an unbelievable melodrama, or the clown in a sidesplitting comedy—any of these within a few hours.

—Bobby Jones

The greedy golfer will go too near and be sucked into his own destruction.

—John L. Low

Every day in every way I am getting better and better and, believe it or not, you did. What Benny wants you to say is simply that every day in every way your golf is getting better. Say it two thousand times and then go out and see what happens.

—John P. Marquand

Too much ambition is a bad thing to have in a bunker.

—Bobby Jones

If you travel first class, you think first class and are more likely to play first class.

—Ray Floyd

Anyone who hasn't been nervous, or hasn't choked somewhere down the line, is an idiot.

—Cary Middlecoff

You have to take this game through so many labyrinths of the mind, past all the traps, like: 'Will my masculinity be threatened if I hit the ball well and still shoot 72?'

—Mac O'Grady

In competition you must be yourself . . . If you're the joking sort, go ahead and joke. If you're the serious sort, there's no need to pretend not to be.

—Harvey Penick,
from *Harvey Penick's Little Red Book*

The excellence of anyone's game depends on self-control.
—Alex Morrison, *A New Way to Better Golf*

For true success, it matters what our goals are. And it matters how we go about attaining them. The means are as important as the ends. How we get there is as important as where we go.
—Young Tom Morris

Concentration comes out of a combination of confidence and hunger.
—Arnold Palmer

The number one guys have to be almost totally self-centered. They have to possess an incredible burning for success. They have to ignore their friends and enemies and sometimes their families and concentrate entirely on winning.

—Frank Beard

Too many people carry the last shot with them. It is a heavy and useless burden.

—Johnny Miller

It's OK to have butterflies. Just get them flying in formation.

—Francisco Lopez

Every great player has learned the two Cs:
how to concentrate and how to maintain
composure.

—Byron Nelson

But the butterflies in the stomach have
hatched, and as we take our stance the line of
the putt wriggles and slips around like a snake
on glass.

—John Updike, on three- and four-footers

Nobody can know what's in my heart. Nobody
can know what I'm thinking. I know what I've
got to do.

—John Daly

All athletes, when they get in pressure situations, revert to what they know. I don't think you are going to revert to mechanics. I think you revert to feel.

—Jack Nicklaus, *Golf Digest*

I have only one goal in golf—to leave it with my sanity.

—Joe Inman

After taking the stance, it is too late to worry. The only thing to do then is to hit the ball.

—Bobby Jones

Be decisive. A wrong decision is generally less disastrous than indecision.

—Bernhard Langer

Golf should make you think, and use your eyes, your intelligence, and your imagination. Variety and precision are more important than power and length.

—Jack Nicklaus

You create your own luck by the way you play. There is no such luck as bad luck. Fate has nothing to do with success or failure, because that is a negative philosophy that indicts one's confidence, and I'll have no part of it.

—Greg Norman

You must attain a neurological and biological serenity in chaos. You cannot let yourself be sabotaged by adrenaline.

—Mac O'Grady

The most rewarding things you do in life are often the ones that look like they cannot be done.

—Arnold Palmer

The other truth about golf spectatorship is
that for today's pros it all comes down to the
putting, and that the difference between a
putt that drops and one that rims the cup,
though teleologically enormous, is intellectually
negligible.

—John Updike

Confidence in golf means being able to
concentrate on the problem at hand with no
outside interference.

—Tom Watson

Golf has probably kept more people sane than
psychiatrists have.

—Harvey Penick

To control his own ball, all alone without
help or hindrance, the golfer must first and
last control himself. At each stroke, the ball
becomes a vital extension, an image of one's
innermost self.

—John Stuart Martin,
The Curious History of the Golf Ball

I'll tell you one thing about chasing a little white
ball. Make what you want out of it, but it's all
on the greens—and half of that's in your head.

—Tom Weiskopf

I accept the fact that I'm going to miss it sometimes. I just hope I miss it where I can find it.

—Fuzzy Zoeller, *The Swing: Mastering the Principles of the Game*

Maintain a childhood enthusiasm for the game of golf.

—Chi-Chi Rodriguez

My ultimate ambition is to be able to afford to retire from the game because it drives me berserk.

—David Feherty

Don't let the bad shots get to you. Don't let yourself become angry. The true scramblers are thick-skinned. And they always beat the whiners.

—Paul Runyan

Sometimes things work out on the golf course and sometimes they don't. Life will go on.

—Greg Norman

Every day I try to tell myself that this is going to be fun today. I try to put myself in a great frame of mind before I go out—then I screw it up on the first shot.

—Johnny Miller

Golf is the only game that pits the player against an opponent, the weather, the minutest details of a large chunk of topography, and his own nervous system, all at the same time.

—Mike Seabrook

Sometimes thinking too much can destroy your momentum.

—Tom Watson

A hundred years of experience has demonstrated that the game is temporary insanity practiced in a pasture.

—Dave Kindred

The first thing you gotta learn about this game, Doc, is it isn't about hitting a little white ball into some yonder hole. It's about inner demons and self-doubt and human frailty and overcoming all that crap.

—Ron Shelton, from his screenplay
for the film *Tin Cup*

There is no shape nor size of body, no awkwardness nor ungainliness, which puts good golf beyond reach. There are good golfers with spectacles, with one eye, with one leg, even with one arm. In golf, while there is life there is hope.

—Sir Walter Simpson, *The Art of Golf*

Thinking instead of acting is the number-one golf disease.

—Sam Snead

It takes years to build up your confidence, but it hardly takes a moment to lose it. Confidence is when you stand over a shot and know you're going to make it because you've done it time and time again.

—Jack Nicklaus

I love to watch *Oprah*, *Geraldo*, all the shows about dysfunctionals. That's my psychoanalysis. I realized I wasn't as bad as I thought.

—Mac O'Grady

The three things I fear most in golf are
lightning, Ben Hogan, and a downhill putt.

—Sam Snead

The person I fear most in the last two rounds is
myself.

—Tom Watson

First tee ball at those things is more daunting
to me than any business deal.

—Donald Trump,
on playing at pro-am tournaments

The number-one thing about trouble is . . .
don't get into more.

—Dave Stockton

I don't derive satisfaction from trying to satisfy other people's expectations. I am not out to prove anything to you or to anybody else. I am out to prove it to me.

—David Duval

It's not artificial and no tricks about it. Either you hit the fairway or you're going to be in trouble.

—Mike Weir

A golfer chokes when he lets anger, doubt, fear, or some other extraneous factors distract him before a shot.
—Dr. Bob Rotella, from *Golf Is Not a Game of Perfect*

Its power as a symbol is so complex and labyrinthine, so capable of lending itself to the psyche of each and every player, that once an attempt like this has begun to comprehend its inner meaning, all bearings may be lost.
—Michael Murphy, on golf, *Golf in the Kingdom*

You seem to forget that luck is a part of the game and a good golfer must be good at all parts of the game.
—Walter Travis, when it was suggested that he lost the US Amateur because of an opponent's luck

Competitive golf is played mainly on a five-and-a-half-inch course, the space between your ears.

—Bobby Jones

In the game of life it's a good idea to have a few early losses, which relieves you of the pressure of trying to maintain an undefeated season.

—Lee Trevino

If I never win a major or never hit another golf ball again, I can look back and say I'm successful. I only need to look at my house to know that. I didn't inherit it . . . I earned it.

—Colin Montgomerie

Relax? How can anybody relax and play golf?
You have to grip the club, don't you?

—Ben Hogan

Give luck a chance to happen.

—Tom Kite

Good players have the power to think while
they are competing. Most golfers are not
thinking even when they believe they are. They
are only worrying.

—Harvey Penick

I'm a strong believer in fate. And I believe it's
not over. Anything is possible.

—Justin Leonard

Try to think where you want to put the ball, not where you don't want it to go.

—Billy Casper

The muttered hint, 'Remember, you have a stroke here,' freezes my joints like a blast from Siberia.

—John Updike

When you play the game for fun, it's fun. When you play for a living, it's a game of sorrows.

—Gary Player

You have the hands, now play with the heart.

—Roberto De Vicenzo, to Seve Ballesteros

Either a wise man will not go into the bunkers, or, being in, he will endure such things as befall him with patience.

—Andrew Lang

In golf you've got two continuously merciless competitors, yourself and the course.

—Tommy Armour

First you've got to be good, but then you've got to be lucky.

—Harry Cooper

Next to the idiotic, the dull unimaginative mind is the best for golf.

—Sir Walter Simpson

If you are going to continue to rely on somebody every time, you never end up doing it yourself.
—Jack Nicklaus, on teachers, *Golf Digest,* 1991

Peter Alliss used to say I hit miracle shots. I never thought that. Miracles don't happen very often; I was hitting those shots all the time.
—Seve Ballesteros

I know how to choke. Given a splinter-thin opportunity to let my side down and destroy my own score, I will seize it. Not only does ice water not run through my veins, but what runs there has a boiling point lower than body temperature.

—John Updike, *Golf Digest*, 1995

One thing about golf is you don't know why you play bad and why you play good.

—George Archer

I used golf as a Zen exercise. I learned that a person who is able to concentrate and focus can do almost anything.

—T-Bone Burnett

I try to be semi-humble. If I started going around saying how good I was, everything would go wrong.

—Johnny Miller

Don't be in such a hurry. That little white ball isn't going to run away from you.

—Patty Berg

Success is a choice; therefore, so is failure.

—Bob Brue

At first a golfer excuses a dismal performance by claiming bad lies. With experience, he covers up with better ones.

—P. Brown

Water creates a neurosis in golfers. The very thought of this harmless fluid robs them of their normal powers of rational thought, turns their legs to jelly, and produces a palsy of the upper limbs.

—Peter Dobereiner

In golf, as in life, the attempt to do something in one stroke that needs two is apt to result in taking three.

—Walter Camp

Pressure is playing for $50 a hole with only $5 in your pocket.

—Lee Trevino

We create success or failure on the course primarily by our thoughts.

—Gary Player

Ask yourself how many shots you would have saved if you never lost your temper, never got down on yourself, always developed a strategy before you hit, and always played within your own capabilities.

—Jack Nicklaus

Golf has its drawbacks. It is possible, by too much of it, to destroy the mind.

—Sir Walter Simpson, *The Art of Golf*

I shot a wild elephant in Africa thirty yards from me, and it didn't hit the ground until it was right at my feet. I wasn't a bit scared. But a four-foot putt scares me to death.

—Sam Snead

I'm about five inches from being an outstanding golfer. That's the distance my left ear is from my right.

—Ben Crenshaw

The clubs were not the problem. My brain was.
—Payne Stewart, on his 1994 season

Serenity is knowing that your worst shot is still pretty good.
—Johnny Miller

CHAPTER 4

HISTORY OF THE GAME

We borrowed golf from Scotland as we borrowed whiskey. Not because it is Scottish, but because it is good.

—Horace Hutchinson

In the homeland of golf, Scots played for centuries on terrain that was entirely natural. These natural links of Scotland form the foundation of the practice of golf architecture even today.

—Geoffrey S. Cornish,
golf architect and writer

Golf is a plague invented by the Calvinistic Scots as a punishment for man's sins. As General Eisenhower discovered, it is easier to end the Cold War or stamp out poverty than to master this devilish pastime.

—James Reston

Scotland is a peculiar land that is the birthplace of golf and sport salmon fishing, a fact that may explain why it is also the birthplace of whisky.

—Henry Beard

Golf is an exercise which is much used by the Gentlemen of Scotland. A large common in which there are several little holes is chosen for the purpose. It is played with leather balls stuffed with feathers; and sticks made somewhat in the form of a handy-wicket.

—Benjamin Rush, American founding father

Here one makes clubs fine and noble.
Play colf with pleasure, not brawls.
Play for a pint or a gallon.
Let the winter be cold and hard,
We play the ball just the same.

—House sign in Haarlem,
The Netherlands, 1650

I think most of the rules of golf stink. They were written by guys who can't even break a hundred.

—Chi-Chi Rodriguez

Ever since golf began—Scottish historians have settled on the year 1100 as a reasonable date of birth—the game has been an enigma.

—Herbert Warren Wind

In golf the cardinal rules are arbitrary and not founded on eternal justice. Equity has nothing to do with the game itself. If founded on eternal justice the game would be deadly dull to watch and play.

—Charles Blair Macdonald

93

Golf was invented by some Scotsman who hit a ball, with a stick, into a hole . . . The game today is exactly the same, except that it now takes some ninety-odd pages of small type to ensure that the ball is hit, with the stick, into the hole . . . without cheating.

—A.S. Graham

From its earliest beginnings, golf has been a gentleman's game—to be played as much for the sake of the game as for the contest.

—Tony Lema

I was playing golf the day
That the Germans landed;
All our troops had run away,

94

All our ships were stranded;
And the thought of England's shame
Altogether spoilt my game.

—Anonymous

Unlike many other sports, golf does not enjoy
the privilege of knowing its exact birthright.

—Ian Morrison, author

When I was in that streak, I didn't do anything
but play golf. That's why I think it was more fun
in our time. It was hard, but people like to be
challenged. They like it hard.

—Byron Nelson, *Golf Digest*

After the Restoration, James Duke of York was sent to Edinburgh, and his favourite pastimes appear to have been torturing of the adherents to the Covenant, and the playing of golf on the Links of Leith.

—John Robertson

Racism in golf reared its head in America as early as 1896. In the second U.S. Open, held that year at Shinnecock Hills, a group of professionals threatened to boycott play if John Shippen, of black and Indian parentage, was allowed to compete . . . Theodore Havemeyer [USGA President] refused to bar him.

—Bud Dufner

In the old days, who wanted to see a pro play? All he did was play when a member wanted a mercenary as his advisor.

—Herb Graffis, famous American golf writer
and administrator

The 1922 U.S. Open was the first USGA event with an admission fee for spectators. In less than four years, thanks to the popularity of Bobby Jones and other players, those fees became the organization's chief source of income.

—*Golf* magazine, December 1994

Old Tom is the most remote point to which
we can carry back our genealogical inquiries
into the golfing style, so that we may virtually
accept him as the common golfing ancestor
who has stamped the features of his style
most distinctly on his descendants.
—Horace Hutchinson, 1900, on Old Tom Morris

According to the Captain of the Honourable
Company of Edinburgh Golfers, striking your
opponent or caddie at St. Andrews, Hoylake,
or Westward Ho! meant that you lost the hole,
except on medal days when it counted as a rub
of the green.

—Herbert Warren Wind

Indoor golf is to be one of the features of the athletic work of many young society girls this winter. They are the younger girls . . . but they have already been exposed to the contagion of golf, and they will prepare . . . to be genuine fanatics by the time their school duties are over.

—*The New York Times*, November 14, 1897

Linksland is the old Scottish word for the earth at the edge of the sea . . . You see, the game comes out of the ocean, just like man himself! Investigate our linksland. Michael, get to know it. I think you'll find it worthwhile.

—Michael Bamberger, from *Stark*

There's a widely held respect for the game, for fellow competitors, and for its history that's very appealing.

—Bob Costas

What golf has of honor, what it has of justice, of fair play, of good fellowship, and sportsmanship—in a word, what is best in golf—is almost surely traceable to the inspiration of the Royal & Ancient.

—Isaac Grainger

CHAPTER 5

HUMBLE BEGINNINGS: FAMOUS PLAYERS ON THEIR GOLFING ORIGINS

I do not recall the first time I hit a golf ball, or hit at one; and as I recall it the game did not make much of an impression on me.

—Bobby Jones

The best year of my life was when I was eleven. I got straight As, had two recesses a day, and the cutest girlfriend, and won thirty-two tournaments that year. Everything's been downhill since.

—Tiger Woods

When I was three . . . my father put my hands
in his and placed them around the shaft of a
cut-down women's golf club. He showed me
the classic overlap, or the Vardon grip . . . and
told me to hit the golf ball . . . 'Hit it hard, boy.
Go find it and hit it again.'

—Arnold Palmer, *A Golfer's Life*

I needed to be pushed. As a youngster I didn't
recognize my true ability or talents . . . Sure, I
said I was going to the golf course, but when
I got my driver's license, man, as soon as I got
out of sight, I took the next left.

—Pat Bradley, LPGA Hall of Famer

It took her at least two years to learn to respect the short game and realize that even the top players have to be able to get down in two from off the green. Then her chipping and putting started to improve, and, of course, her scoring did.

—Betsy Rawls, on Mickey Wright

I was so poor, I grew up under a sign that said, 'Made in Taiwan.'

—Chi-Chi Rodriguez

My family was so poor they couldn't afford any kids. The lady next door had me.

—Lee Trevino

I had played poorly for two years and started thinking, 'Gee, maybe I'll do something else.' Then I saw my friends going to work every day and realized that my life wasn't so bad. I've been more patient with my golf ever since.

—Steve Pate

Golf, like measles, should be caught young, for, if postponed to riper years, the results may be serious.

—P.G. Wodehouse, *A Mixed Threesome*

Being left-handed isn't really so different anymore. It's not like when I was a kid.

—Mike Weir

105

If I'm going to play golf, I might as well play for the money.

—Arnold Palmer, upon turning pro

The first time I grabbed a golf club, I knew that I'd do it for the rest of my life.

—Michelle Wie

One of the things that my parents have taught me is never listen to other people's expectations. You should live your own life and live up to your own expectations, and those are the only things I really care about.

—Tiger Woods

If you really want to get better at golf, go back and take it up at a much earlier age.

—Thomas Mulligan

When Tiger was six months old, he would sit in our garage, watching me hit balls into a net. He had been assimilating his golf swing. When he got out of a high chair, he had a golf swing.

—Earl Woods

From the time you're a junior, adults keep telling you about patience and hard work and using your head, but until you've been knocked down a few times and have to get back on your feet all by yourself, you probably haven't learned the lessons.

—Mike Weir

In the summer of 1968, a young golfer from Texas experienced something that would forever change his life. Not only did I fall in love with formal tournament competition, but I was enraptured with so many other facets of the game: the different courses, the people, the history and traditions.

—Ben Crenshaw

I used to sling the old golf club quite a distance. Tony (my brother) and I used to be dreadful. We would spend twenty minutes or longer trying to retrieve a club one of us had thrown into a tree.

—Laura Davies, LPGA Tour player

People begin playing for many reasons—exercise, because a friend plays, an injury has made some more physical game impossible, business contacts or often because the game is played in such beautiful surroundings.

—Michael Hobbs, *Golf for the Connoisseur*

When I joined the tour in 1964, I told my wife I wanted to play five years. Instead, I've played five careers.

—George Archer

I'd probably been up to 250, but I just happened to be at 215 at the time. I'd probably be the fat lady in a circus right now if it hadn't been for golf. It kept me on the course and out of the refrigerator.

—Kathy Whitworth, on her portly youth

People think growing up in the hills was a handicap I had to overcome. In a lot of ways it gave me [an] . . . advantage that has lasted me to this day. Just like with that stick, I'd have to overcompensate for just about everything; stick for clubs, acorns for balls . . .

—Sam Snead

Of all the golfers in the world I cannot believe that anyone will make a greater impact upon the championships than this very tough, determined young man. The world is at his feet and he is only 21 years of age.

—Pat Ward Thomas, on Jack Nicklaus

111

Why do I love kids so much? Because I never was a kid myself. I was too poor to be a child, so I never really had a childhood. The biggest present I ever got was a marble.

—Chi-Chi Rodriguez

Whenever we left our apartment to go play in Canada or Australia, we couldn't afford to keep the apartment. So every year we had to get our stuff and pile it in a storage locker for $50 a month. Then we'd find another apartment.

—Mike Weir

I learned by copying. My father used to take Roger and me to watch golf when we were youngsters, and I tried to copy the good players' rhythm. Then, when I began playing fairly well, I played a lot with Roger and his friends from Oxford.

—Joyce Wethered, leading women's golfer in the 1920s and 1930s

I owe much to having seen her play when I was just coming to understand golf a little. She put the kindling in the fire that was beginning to burn.

—Glenna Collett Vare, on Alexa Stirling

I fancy that having at first played the game almost entirely by the light of nature he [Gene Sarazen] took to thinking about it. That is a thing that has almost got to happen to any good young golfer at some time.

—Bernard Darwin

Forget the PGA Tour. There's no money in it.

—Titanic Thompson,
advice to Lee Trevino in 1966

CHAPTER 6

THE DIFFICULTY, NATURE, VALUES, AND CHARACTER-BUILDING SPIRIT OF THE GAME

Is my friend in the bunker or is the bastard on the green?

—Anonymous

It's a slow process. You can't go from struggling, having trouble holing putts, to making everything just like that. If I keep making good putts here and there, feeling confident, consistent over the ball, it's going to be important.

—Sergio Garcia

It takes six years to make a golfer: three to learn the game, then another three to unlearn all that you have learned in the first three years. You might be a golfer when you arrive at that stage, but more likely you are just starting.

—Walter Hagen

Golf is the cruelest game, because eventually it will drag you out in front of the whole school, take your lunch money and slap you around.

—Rick Reilly

I am the most fortunate, failed golfer in the world.

—Tom Coyne

'Who is the best lefthand player you ever saw?'
said Mr. Bliss, himself a lefthander and playing
the game of his life. 'Never saw one that was
worth a damn,' Harry Vardon replied.
—Michael Hobbs

Stroke play is my second favorite form of golf,
and by quite a long way. It is not the play itself
that puts me off, it is the task of marking a
card.
—Peter Dobereiner

Have you ever actually listened to golfers talking to each other? Looked good starting out . . . Better direction than last time . . . Who's away? . . . It sounds like visitors' day at a home for the criminally insane.

—Peter Andrews

It taught me perseverance, it taught me not to cheat—no easy thing for a boy when he's two down and his ball is deep in the woods.

—James Reston

I don't enjoy playing video golf because there is nothing to throw.

—Paul Azinger

My game is so bad I've got to hire three caddies—one to walk the left rough, one for the right rough, and one down the middle. And the one in the middle doesn't have much to do.

—Dave Hill

Do I have to know rules and all that crap? Then forget it.

—John Daly

The biggest liar in the world is the golfer who claims that he plays the game merely for exercise.

—Tommy Bolt

Two things I take very seriously in life. My golf game and my relationship with God. Neither one is simple.

—Cheryl Ladd

It's been a funny week. It took me three days to play 18 holes.

—Hale Irwin

One reward golf has given me, and I shall always be thankful for it, is introducing me to some of the world's most picturesque, tireless, and bald-faced liars.

—Rex Lardner

If you are going to throw a club, it is important to throw it ahead of you, down the fairway, so you don't have to waste energy going back to pick it up.

—Tommy Bolt

If profanity had an influence on the flight of the ball, the game of golf would be played far better than it is.

—Horace Hutchinson

The most exquisitely satisfying act in the world of golf is that of throwing a club. The full backswing, the delayed wrist action, the flowing follow-through, followed by that unique whirring sound, reminiscent only of a passing flock of starlings, are without parallel in sport.

—Henry Longhurst

Would that I could hand on unimpaired the great game as it was my good fortune to know it.

—Charles Blair Macdonald

A great deal of unnecessarily bad golf is played in this world.

—Harry Vardon

It's how you deal with failure that determines how you achieve success.

—David Feherty

I don't fear death, but I sure don't like those three-footers for par.

—Chi-Chi Rodriguez

Golf may be played on Sunday, not being a game within view of the law, but being a form of moral effort.

—Stephen Leacock

Tommy [Bolt] threw clubs with class.

—Don January

I'm hitting the woods just great, but I am having a terrible time hitting out of them.

—Harry Toscano

Many play golf, and one odd effect of that pursuit is that they return to work manifestly stupider than they were. It is, I think, the company of other golfers.

—G.W. Lyttleton

With any other sport or pastime golf compares favorably.

—Sir Walter Simpson

As good a golfer as Tiger is, he's a better person.

—Earl Woods

Tell me honestly: do you know anyone who truly likes to play golf? Oh, I suppose there are some people who derive pleasure from golf just as there are certain kinds of individuals who enjoy being snapped in the rib cage with knotted towels.

—Peter Andrews

There were no 'two Gerald Fords,' there was no other agenda, no secret life. An avid golfer to the end, he would never move his ball to improve his lie when no one was looking. To me that was the central theme of his character.

—David Hume Kennerly

When you lose your swing, you might just as well quit walking around in the sun and get in the shade.

—Jimmy Demaret

People who are great in other sports, whom I have worked with, always say that golf is the toughest game they've ever played because it's not just athleticism that enables them to become great. Golf is far more than that.

—David Leadbetter

CHAPTER 7

INSTRUCTION

Golf, more than most games, has a number of clichés, often successfully disguised as 'tips.' Watch out.

—Kathy Whitworth

If you have a good short game you have a powerful ally.

—Nick Price

I think I'm the only president whose handicap has gone down while he's in been in office. It's only because I've gotten to play with all these pros and other good golfers, and they give me all this good advice.

—President Bill Clinton

Frank, either you have to get better soon or quit telling people I'm your teacher.
>
> —Dave Marr, to Pro Football
> Hall of Famer Frank Gifford

The reason the pro tells you to keep your head down is so you can't see him laughing.
>
> —Phyllis Diller

Many shots are spoiled at the last instant by efforts to add a few more yards.
>
> —Bobby Jones

You drive for show and putt for dough.
>
> —Al Balding

Give me a man with big hands, big feet, and no brains, and I will make a golfer out of him.
—Walter Hagen

There are three ways of learning golf: by study, which is the most wearisome; by imitation, which is the more fallacious; and by experience, which is the most bitter.
—Robert Browning

Being a left-hander is a big advantage. No one knows enough about your game to mess you up with advice.

—Bob Charles

Instruction

You'll get better results—and often more distance—if you swing at eighty percent effort.

—Ernie Els

Imagine the ball has little legs, and chop them off.

—Henry Cotton

If you think your hands are more important in your golf swing than your legs, try walking a hole on your hands.

—Gary Player

If a lot of people gripped a knife and fork the way they do a golf club, they'd starve to death.

—Sam Snead

133

The most important single move in establishing your tempo and rhythm is your takeaway. It sets the beat for everything that comes later. Strive on every shot to move the club back as *deliberately* as possible, consistent with swinging it [back] rather than taking it [back].

—Jack Nicklaus

The difference between a good golf shot and a bad one is the same as the difference between a beautiful and a plain woman—a matter of millimeters.

—Ian Fleming

Make the hard ones look easy and the easy ones look hard.

—Walter Hagen

The ultimate judge of your swing is the flight of the ball.

—Ben Hogan

Placing the ball in the right position for the next shot is eighty percent of winning golf.

—Ben Hogan

It's often necessary to hit a second shot to really appreciate the first one.

—Henry Beard

It is nothing new or original to say that golf is played one stroke at a time. But it took me many years to realize it.

—Bobby Jones

The biggest disaster shots in the game are usually tee shots.

—Raymond Floyd

Mine was, and remains, the antithesis of a 'mechanical' golf swing.

—Arnold Palmer

Don't swing the club, let the club swing you.

—Leslie Nielsen

It seems to me the more loft there is on a club, the harder it is to play. Why, I don't know.

—Bobby Jones

Feel at ease, lack worry, and no guessing as you hit the ball.

—Walter Hagen

Reverse every natural instinct and do the opposite of what you are inclined to do, and you will probably come very close to having a perfect golf swing.

—Ben Hogan

You're not going to find a golf swing in a book.

—Tony Lema

You don't hit anything on the backswing, so
why rush it?

—Doug Ford

I improve and that is the key to my golf
swing . . . I think consistency is the key. That
comes from the golf swing. I can hit the ball
longer and straighter than I've ever done
before, so that's a key factor.

—Vijay Singh

Love and putting are mysteries for the
philosopher to solve. Both subjects are beyond
golfers.

—Tommy Armour

I've been squeezing the club so hard the cow is screaming.

—J.C. Snead

The woods are full of long hitters.

—Jerry Barber

A perfectly straight shot with a big club is a fluke!

—Jack Nicklaus

Golf is played with the arms.

—Sam Snead

Only one golfer in a thousand grips the club lightly enough.

—Johnny Miller

Every good golfer keeps his left hand leading the clubhead through impact.

—Lee Trevino

The ball's got to stop somewhere. It might as well be in the bottom of the hole.

—Lee Trevino

Instruction

Hit the ball up to the hole . . . You meet a better class of person there.

—Ben Hogan

Concentrate on hitting the green. The cup will come to you.

—Cary Middlecoff

Ninety percent of putts that are short don't go in.

—Yogi Berra

Gimme: an agreement between two losers who can't putt.

—Jim Bishop

Half of golf is fun; the other half is putting.
                              —Peter Dobereiner

Keep close count of your nickels and dimes, stay away from whiskey, and never concede a putt.

                                        —Sam Snead

Bobby Jones told me he used to run back to Stewart Maiden . . . for lessons. He said that when he learned to be able to correct himself on the golf course, control his game and do it himself, that's when he became a good player.
                              —Jack Nicklaus

It may not be out of place here to say that I never won a major championship until I learned to play golf against something, not somebody. And that something was par.

—Bobby Jones

Every shot in golf should be played as a shot at some clearly defined target. All players realize this when they are playing a shot to the green . . . But what many of them forget is the shot off the tee should also be aimed at the target down the fairway.

—Craig Wood

I rarely aimed at the flag. I aimed at the spot where I had the best birdie opportunity.

—Ben Hogan

Give me a man with a fast backswing and a fat wallet.

—Golf hustler's saying

You get rewarded at the bottom of the club by what you do at the top end.

—Jerry Barber

Always—and I mean ALWAYS—tee the ball on par-3 holes, or any other time play your opening shot with an iron.

—Jack Nicklaus

The ideal build for a golfer would be strong hands, big forearms, thin neck, big thighs, and a flat chest. He looks like Popeye.

—Gary Player

Rhythm is best expressed in any swing directed at a cigar stump or a dandelion head.

—Grantland Rice

If you feel like you're just trying to get the ball into play, it's easier to avoid the urge to swing too hard.

—Neal Lancaster

If your adversary is a hole or two down, there is no serious cause for alarm in his complaining of a severely sprained wrist, or an acute pain, resembling lumbago, which checks his swing.
—Horace Hutchinson

Golf demands a complex series of movements to maximize the athlete's latent energy and apply it to the object to be moved.
—Jim McLean

CHAPTER 8:

CADDIES, GALLERIES, FAMILY, AND MEDIA

Without the people, I'd be playing in front of trees for a couple hundred dollars.

—Fuzzy Zoeller

I know I'm getting better at golf because I'm hitting fewer spectators.

—President Gerald Ford

I enjoy the 'oohs' and the 'ahhs' for the gallery when I hit my drives. But I'm getting pretty tired of the 'awws' and 'uhhs' when I miss the putt.

—John Daly

With the huge excited crowd surging all around him, it is only natural that the player should come in for a good deal of buffeting about. It may come as a surprise to many people to know after a big tournament my ankles and shins are black and blue.

—Harry Vardon

He [Ben Hogan]'s the only player I have ever known to get an ovation from the fans on the practice tee. I've seen him playing practice rounds before a tournament and half the gallery was made up of other professionals.

—Tommy Bolt

I like it loud, and when you've got people pulling for you like that, you want to play good. The fans have been great everywhere I've gone.

—John Daly

After all the noise and clamor . . . after the clubs are cleaned and stacked . . . the silence which follows the last round played seems strange, bewildering, yet wonderfully peaceful. However, this silence, to me, often reverberates with the roars and the applause of the fans who followed me for so many years.

—Walter Hagen

Another great trick of well-meaning friends in
a gallery following your match is that of telling
you how you should play your shot . . . That is
the worst pest of all because they offer advice,
unsolicited as it may be, in such a way that it
great irritates you.

—Francis Ouimet

I have a tough time looking at the fans because
of the things I've done. I don't look at myself
as being as good enough to talk to them.

—John Daly

It wasn't dangerous enough. I'd rather be in the
gallery and get hit by a ball.

—Jerry Seinfeld, on his only round of golf ever

Someone who turns up at the first tee on time and sober.

—Ernie Els, describing a good caddie

It is a game of tradition, one we'd like to maintain. Plus, I don't think their long legs look very good.

—Reg Murphy, USGA President, on why he disallowed caddies to wear shorts during the 1994 US Open

Remember the basic rule: Make friends with your caddie and the game will make friends with you.

—Stephen Potter

[Bill Clinton] told me that he caddied in the same group with me in the Hot Springs Open. That's why I voted for him, because he was a caddy.

—Tommy Bolt

The professional [caddie] is a reckless, feckless creature. In the golfing season in Scotland he makes money all day and spends it all the night. His sole loves are golf and whiskey.

—Horace Hutchinson

If a permanent caddie is heroin, if you're going to break out in a cold sweat because you don't have him, then you'd better get one.

—Frank Beard

153

The only time I talk on a golf course is to my caddie. And then only to complain when he gives me the wrong club.

—Seve Ballesteros

I know you can be fined for throwing a club, but I want to know if you can get fined for throwing a caddie?

—Tommy Bolt

If your caddie coaches you on the tee, 'Hit it down the left side with a little draw,' ignore him. All you do on the tee is try not to hit the caddie.

—Jim Murray

The Royal Hong Kong Club caddies hit the nail on the head; their term for golf: 'Hittee ball, say damn.'

—Dick Anderson

The first bunker lesson I ever got was from my dad, Neels, and it was real simple. He told me to thump the sand behind the ball with the back of my sand wedge and finish my swing.

—Ernie Els

Golf is played by twenty million mature American men whose wives think they are out there having fun.

—Jim Bishop

155

Rock-a-bye, baby—till father comes home;
Father's off golfing and mother's alone; He
phoned me this morning—he wanted his
cleek; Perhaps he'll be home again, sometime
next week.

>   —Mother Goose on the Links, 1909

When I come back in the next life, I want to
come back as a golf pro's wife. She wakes
up every morning at the crack of ten and is
faced with her first major decision of the day:
whether to have breakfast in bed or in the
hotel coffee shop.

>   —Sam Sikes

Playing with your spouse on the golf course runs almost as great a marital risk as getting caught playing with someone else's anywhere else.

—Peter Andrews

The place of the father in the modern suburban family is a very small one, particularly if he plays golf.

—Betrand Russell

It's nice to look down the fairway and see your mother on the left and your father on the right. You know that no matter whether you hook or slice it, somebody is going to be there to kick it back in the fairway.

—Larry Nelson

157

A golfer needs a loving wife to whom he can describe the day's play through the long evening.

—P.G. Wodehouse

I motivated myself by thinking of my family . . . If I play well, I feel like I can justify being away from them—it's okay to leave them that week. If I don't play well, then I feel like I've wasted time I could have spent with them.

—Nancy Lopez

It is a sport in which the whole American family can participate—fathers and mothers, sons and daughters alike. It offers healthy respite from daily toil, refreshment of body and mind.

—President Dwight D. Eisenhower

My dad gave me the best golf advice I ever received, which was to have fun. That's the reason why, when I practice, I'm always having fun and enjoying it.

—Phil Mickelson

I tell him the golf game is a gentleman's game. I point out . . . John McEnroe playing Jimmy Connors in tennis and him cursing and throwing his racket. I tell him not to do it, because it will ruin my reputation as a parent. I will not have a spoiled child.

—Kutilda Woods, Tiger Woods' mother

I started golf at 8 . . . He [Dad] and Mom
sacrificed all the time . . . They would go
without, so I could have three new balls or
socks. My wonderful parents gave me the
opportunity to compete with the best and get
the experience I needed to be successful.
                                        —Nancy Lopez

He put his arm around me and said, 'Palsy-
walsy, you and I are going to make a lot of
money.' I've steered clear of agents since.
                                        —Bob Goalby

The men and women who play the game know
me, and I know them.
                                        —Dick Enberg

I don't resent the media. I get disappointed sometimes. They've got their job to do . . . I've got my job to do. They'll sit back some day in years to come and say, 'Well, geez, I was wrong.' They will. I know they will.

—Greg Norman, on being labeled a choker

I like the press room because you can always get something good to eat and drink there.

—Rocky Thompson

I have come to understand and appreciate writers much more recently since I started working on a book last fall. Before that, I thought golf writers got up every morning, played a round of golf, had lunch, showed up for our last three holes and then went to dinner.

—Phil Mickelson

. . . while with long strokes and short
strokes we tend to the goal,
The pond'rous club upon the ball
Descend
Involved in dust th' exulting orb
Ascends.
  —Thomas Mathison, 1743, from *The Goff*, the
              first golf book ever written

Bumpy greens don't bother me anymore,
since I've become an analyst. I don't see the
problem.

                                —David Feherty

It was a great honor to be inducted into the Hall of Fame. I didn't know they had a caddie division.

—Bob Hope

An honest and natural slum dialect is more tolerable than the attempt of a phonetically untaught person to imitate the vulgar dialect of the golf club.

—George Bernard Shaw

I tell the lady scorekeepers that if they can hear me cuss, they're standing too close. They've got to realize they're not at a church social.

—Dave Hill

I've got a lot of people rooting for me because there are more poor people than rich people.
—Lee Trevino

I go to sleep when I watch golf on television.
—George Archer

This [guy] is going to drive over a golf course! Oh, no! If he had drove over the green, I would have had to hang up and get involved with the chase. That would have been just disrespect.
—Bill Murray, watching a police chase on television

165

If you want to take long walks, take long walks. If you want to hit things with a stick, hit things with a stick. But there's no excuse for combining the two and putting the results on TV. Golf is not so much a sport as an insult to lawns.

—*National Lampoon*

Whether I'm shooting 10-under or 10-over I have to realize people have come a long way to see me play. I can't be back-handing putts.

—John Daly

Q: Thirteen? How the hell did you make 13
on a par-5?
Arnold Palmer: Missed a 12-footer for 12.
                                        —Arnold Palmer

I feel like I committed a crime—like I was doing
something very bad.
                              —Seve Ballesteros, on the
                        media's criticism for his bad play

It's gotten to the point where you can't tell race
car drivers from professional golfers.
                    —Lee Trevino, on patch advertisements
                                        worn by golfers

Unless you're able to comprehend the pressures of working for your paycheck each week, I don't know if you can have a true appreciation for the game . . . and how you can go from the top of the mountain to flat on your face.

—Dan Patrick

Golf is one of the easiest sports to get in a player's face. When I'm done, you have to get through the crowd—to get to the locker room. He runs out of the locker room. I think it's a little simpler.

—Fred Couples, comparing his experience with crowds to Michael Jordan's

I think they need to look at their own lives before they use that pen. I'm sure a lot of those guys in the media don't have perfect lives.

> —John Daly, on the media

How about Byron Nelson winning the Byron Nelson?

> —Skip Bayless, on Jack Nicklaus winning the Masters at age 46, and Ray Floyd winning the US Open at age 43

169

There is one thing in this world that is dumber than playing golf. That is watching someone else play golf. What do you actually get to see? Thirty-seven guys in polyester slacks squinting in the sun. Doesn't that set your blood racing?
—Peter Andrews

One of life's great mysteries is just what do golfers think they are playing at. But even more mysterious is what these spectators who traipse around golf courses are looking for.
—Michael Parkinson

Better tournament golf scoring was particularly
due to the Depression because it induced
thousands of urchins who might otherwise
have been playing baseball or annoying their
parents to earn an honest dollar by caddying.
—Noel F. Bush, *The New Yorker*, 1937

Guarantee me three million dollars a year and
you can scream, yell, or spit on my ball when
I'm putting. Because even if I miss, I get paid.
—Lee Trevino

CHAPTER 9:

WOMEN IN GOLF

Look like a woman but play like a man.
>—Jan Stephenson

I've got no objection to women coming into our game if they are good enough.
>—Ian Woosnam

When we complain about conditions, we're just bitches. But when the men complain, people think, 'Well, it really must be hard.'
>—Betsy King, on golf's double standard

In my fifty-seven years of golf, this hole in one is my first ever. To think how many balls I have hit in my life—I was running out of time.
>—Louise Suggs

Q: Are you a golfer?
Hurd: I don't think so, but I believe that they will want me inside to receive the championship cup.

—Dorothy Hurd, in response to an official blocking her way to the awards ceremony after she won the 1909 British Ladies' Championship

We played all our competitions off men's tees. We played country matches off men's tees, we played our county championship off men's tees, we played our championships off of men's tees. What do they do now? They play from the up women's tees.

—Enid Wilson

We were always taught to swing slow with good tempo. But you have to have some acceleration throughout the swing. I think that's where a lot of women go wrong. They should try to whack it a few times and see what happens.

—Helen Alfredsson

There are no more set standards in golf. You don't have to be twenty-five to turn pro. You just have to feel like I do, have a burning inside for the game.

—Christie Kerr, on why she turned down a scholarship to Stanford to turn pro

When you step on the first tee it doesn't matter what you look like. Being pretty, ugly, or semi-ugly has no effect on the golf ball. It doesn't hurt your five-iron if you're pretty.
—Laura Baugh, on her good looks

I may not be the prettiest girl in the world, but I'd like to see Bo Derek look like a 10 after playing 18 holes of golf in 100-degree weather.
—Jan Stephenson

I don't like the idea of golf widows. I was raised to believe I could do anything a man can do.

—Jane Seymour

Women should rely upon their woods more, without fear of being criticized. We're after results and whatever club will put us where we want to be is the club to use.

—Mickey Wright

I simply swing at the ball with the one idea of hitting it . . . The old idea was to hit the ball—few attempts were made at theorizing—and I'm not too sure it wasn't a blessed good idea.

—Dorothy Hurd

The early golf swing was more or less just a swing. Babe [Zaharias] brought the swing and a hit to the game. She got people, especially women, power-minded.

—Patty Berg

I'm not a heavy bettor. I bet for Cokes and stuff. I choke when I play for five dollars.

—Nancy Lopez

If I could go back in time and you asked me whether I took it for granted, the answer would be, 'No.' But deep down, I always thought I would play that good my whole career without any road bumps.

—Karrie Webb

How on earth any of us managed to hit a ball, in the outrageous garments which fashion decreed we should wear, is one of the great unsolved mysteries.

—Mabel Stringer

I used to think pressure was standing over a four-foot putt knowing I had to make it. I learned that real pressure was sixty-five people waiting for their food with only thirty minutes left on their lunch break.

—Amy Alcott, on working as a waitress

I am not talking about ladies' golf because strictly speaking, there is no such thing as ladies' golf—only good or bad golf played by a member of either sex.

—Joyce Wethered

It was one of the greatest thrills of my life. I remember she was wearing tennis shoes and outdistancing the other ladies by twenty yards.

—Paul Azinger, on the time he caddied for Mickey Wright

Paul Azinger wins a tournament and his wife is there on the 18th green with hugs and kisses. Could you imagine me hugging and kissing my woman lover at the conclusion of my last tournament win? Well, that's what you'll see at my next one.

—Muffin Spencer-Devlin

The only thing I like about that number is that it's a good score to turn in for nine holes.

—Liselotte Neumann, on turning 30

Once last year after I'd won four events, someone asked me, 'What kind of year are you having?' Ever hear of a pitcher with a 20-4 record asked what kind of year he's having?
—Betsy King

For a long while, my son thought only women played golf.
—Judy Rankin

Most difficult of all is trying to be a 'good sport.' You are compelled to do many things you don't give two hoots about. To go to parties when you just long to be in bed, to be nice to all sorts of people, ask all sorts of favors.
—Glenna Collett Vare

The only area where I have ever experienced discrimination is athletics. Growing up, I couldn't play Little League baseball or be on the high school golf team simply because I was a girl. But that's changing.

—Betsy King

Let us examine the proposition that women golfers are people. It requires an effort to adjust to this idea, for, ever since the beheading of the first woman golfer, Mary Queen of Scots, the golf world has openly regretted that the practice didn't start a trend.

—Peter Dobereiner

I'm kind of in between a goody-goody and a rebel. I'm not bad, but I'm not good either. I'm a little crazy.

—Michelle Wie

In 1587, golf's first famous woman player [Mary Queen of Scots] was convicted and beheaded. Women's golf went into something of a decline after that.

—Rhonda Glenn

If it weren't for golf, I'd be waiting on this table instead of sitting at it.

—Judy Rankin

I have not played golf with anyone, man or woman, amateur or professional, who made me feel so utterly outclassed.
                    —Bobby Jones, on Joyce Wethered

CHAPTER 10

CLUBS

Clubs

The best wood in most amateurs' bags is the pencil.
—Chi-Chi Rodriguez

Although golf was originally restricted to wealthy, overweight Protestants, today it's open to anybody who owns hideous clothing.
—Dave Barry

If you think it's hard to meet new people, try picking up the wrong golf ball.
—Jack Lemmon

Selecting a putter is like selecting a wife. To each his own.
—Ben Hogan

All golfers fear the one-iron. It has no angle, no loft. The one-iron is a confidence-crusher, a fear trip, an almost guarantee of shame, failure, dumbness, and humiliation if you ever use it in public.

—Hunter S. Thompson

Being slave to the game is one thing. Being a cringing captive to one warped club is something else.

—Grantland Rice

The golf cart has opened the eyes of
Americans to the need for more truly universal
design that not only improves the lives of
people with disabilities, but the lives of us all.
—George H.W. Bush

I may be the only golfer never to have broken
a single putter, if you don't count the one I
twisted into a loop and threw into a bush.
—Thomas Boswell

I've thrown or broken a few clubs in my day. In
fact, I guess at one time or another I probably
held distance records for every club in the bag.
—Tommy Bolt

To many, Bolt's putter has spent more time in
the air than Lindbergh.
                    —Jimmy Demaret, on Tommy Bolt

Bolt (to caddie): Why are you handing me a
3-iron for a shot of less than 100 yards?

Caddie (nervously): Because it's the only club
left.
                    —Tommy Bolt

Why am I using a new putter? Because the last
one didn't float too well.
                    —Craig Stadler

There are many ways to punish a putter, such as burning, rusting, and drowning, but the most torturous is to drag it along the pavement out of the door of a fast-moving vehicle.
> —Dan Jenkins, demonstrating one of his *Ten Basic Rules for Happy Putting*

If you ask me, I don't think anything should be illegal . . . golf equipment, that is.
> —John Daly

The sound of a golf ball on a skull is remarkably like that of two blocks of wood being knocked together.
> —John Updike, *The Golf Book*

If it was good enough for Hogan, it's good enough for me.

>   —Steve Elkington, on why
>   he used metal spikes

The modern player has grown so accustomed to having a special club for every conceivable stroke, that he fails to realize how much of his vaunted skill is due to the science of the club-maker.

>   —Robert Browning

'Play it as it lies' is one of the fundamental dictates of golf. The other is: 'Wear it if it clashes.'

>   —Henry Beard

Claude Harmon not only taught me most of
what I know about the golf swing, he took me
out of Argyle socks.

—Dave Marr

Fashions come and go in golf clubs as they do
in clothes and often what is hailed as the latest
thing is only a revival of what was all the rage
fifty years ago.

—Henry Longhurst

The most important item was the plus fours, a kind of knickers that had to hang exactly right if they were to make the wearer look like Gene Sarazen or Walter Hagen, Is not the guy who put on his mother's bloomers by mistake.
—Richard Armour, *Golf Is a Four Letter Word*

Baffling late-life discovery: Golfers wear those awful clothes on purpose.

—Herb Caen

I'd give up golf if I didn't have so many sweaters.

—Bob Hope

Winning is only part of the thing. I wanted people to enjoy seeing me, and I figured if I had fun, they'd have fun.
—Jimmy Demaret, on his colorful wardrobe

I'll have to go shopping. I don't think I have any more clean shirts.
—Mark McCumber, on making his first PGA Tour cut in two years

By the time a man can afford to lose a golf ball, he can't hit it that far.
—Lewis Grizzard

Sports gear purchases are about all that's keeping the fragile US economy alive, and you'd have to get into America's Cup yachting or cross-country airplane racing to find a sport that needs more gear than golf.

—P.J. O'Rourke

Some people say it's a 3-iron/4-iron, but I say it's the secret to a happy life.

—Dan Jenkins, in response to being asked what a 7-wood is, *Golf with the Boss*

I think they should ban all drivers. Just use irons.

—Jose Maria Olazabal

The only thing a golfer needs is more daylight.
—Ben Hogan, on new equipment

The sport isn't like any other where a player can take out all that is eating him on an opponent. In golf, it's strictly you against your clubs.
—Bobby Rosburg

Golf is played with a number of striking implements more intricate in shape than those used in any form of recreation except dentistry.
—E.V. Knox

Some people think the new metal shafts are a great improvement over the old wooden ones. I have tried both and I would do just as well with a rhubarb or asparagus.

—Rube Goldberg, *Left-Handed Golf Courses: Our Greatest Need*

You know the old rule: He who has the fastest cart never has to play a bad lie.

—Mickey Mantle

It's a marriage. If I had to choose between my wife and my putter, well, I'd miss her.

—Gary Player

You have to put your putter out to pasture
every so often, let it eat and get fat so it can
get more birdies.

—Greg Norman

I curse the day the head of my putter fell off.
It's kind of like losing one of your best friends.

—Nick Price

The fact is all golfers are equipment junkies
and professional golfers are the worst of the
lot. They'll do anything to find the perfect putter
even though they'll insist no such instrument
exists.

—Dave Marr

Titleist has offered me a big contract not to play its balls.

—Bob Hope

The winds were blowing 50 mph and gusting to 70. I hit a par-3 with my hat.

—Chi-Chi Rodriguez

Why do I wear a red sport shirt on Sundays? Well, if I play bad on the last round of a tournament and cut my throat, it blends.

—Lee Trevino

In the USA a number of first-class golfers take as long to choose a wife as a club. Sometimes they make the wrong choice in each case.

—Dai Rees

The last thing you want to do is shoot 80 wearing tartan trousers.

—Ian Poulter

I played nine holes with the new short-distance ball. Playing a match with it is like two boxers fighting with pillows.

—Sam Snead

You begin to get the idea that maybe golf manufacturers are out of control when you find out they are making clubs and balls out of components used in nuclear weapons and bulletproof vests.

—E.M. Swift

I feel calm in calm colors. I don't want people to watch the way I dress. I want people to watch the way I play.

—Seve Ballesteros

Nobody else is that stupid.
   —Rocky Thompson, on how he knew that he
      was the only player using a 54-inch driver

The game of golf would lose a great deal if
croquet mallets and billiard cues were allowed
on the putting green.
                              —Ernest Hemingway

Always keep in mind that if God didn't want
man to have mulligans, golf balls wouldn't
come three to a sleeve.
                              —Dan Jenkins

The trouble that most of us find with the modern matched sets of clubs is that they don't really seem to know any more about the game than the old ones did.

—Robert Browning

The other day I broke 70. That's a lot of clubs.

—Anonymous

Not orange. That's tangerine.

—Doug Sanders, to a spectator commenting on his orange outfit

CHAPTER 11

PRACTICE AND PREPARATION

The most valuable time to practice is right after your round, when your mistakes are fresh in your mind.

—Tom Watson

I decided I'm either going to work my ass off or just be an average guy on this Tour. I don't want to be average.

—John Daly

Knowledge, like a sharpened razor, shaves those hardest-to-get strokes and smoothes the rough edges of your game.

—Shawn Humphries,
Two Steps to a Perfect Golf Swing

There is no movement in the golf swing so difficult that it cannot be made even more difficult by careful study and diligent practice.

—Thomas Boswell

They may be able to beat me, but they can't out-practice me.

—Jerry Barber

Swinging at daisies is like playing electric guitar with a tennis racket: if it were that easy, we could all be Jerry Garcia. The ball changes everything.

—Michael Bamberger

It is the constant and undying hope for improvement that makes golf so exquisitely worth the playing.

—Bernard Darwin

Overall I hope I can still improve.

—David Duval, after shooting a 59 at the 1999 Bob Hope Classic

There's no secret to taking your game to the next level. I did it by getting back to basics.

—Ernie Els

A driving range is the place where golfers go to get all the good shots out of their system.

—Henry Beard

You must work very hard to become a natural golfer.

—Gary Player

I worked as hard to perfect my golf game as any other fellow would work in his brokerage office, in his job as a mechanic in a garage, as a lawyer or a traveling salesman.

—Walter Hagen, *The Walter Hagen Story*

It's a funny thing, the more I practice the luckier I get.

—Gary Player

I used to go to the driving range to practice driving without slicing. Now I go to the driving range to practice slicing without swearing.
—Bruce Lansky

You hear stories about me beating my brains out practicing, but . . . I was enjoying myself. I couldn't wait to get up in the morning so I could hit balls. When I'm hitting the ball where I want, hard and crisply, it's a joy that very few people experience.

—Ben Hogan

What a shame to waste those great shots on the practice tee. I'd be afraid of finding out what I was doing wrong.
> —Walter Hagen, on practice

First thing you have to do is get a room with blackout curtains. Start with full wedge shots. The window won't break. You can pretty much go through your short irons and not break the window.
> —Andrew Magee, describing how to practice in motel rooms

If you are only practicing those things that will be successful for you, then you cannot fail to improve.

—Jim Hardy, *The Plane Truth for Golfers*

No matter how good you get you can always get better and that's the exciting part.

—Tiger Woods

I have never been a heavy practicer from the standpoint of just hitting balls. I thought hitting balls in preparation for playing, and finding out how your swing was working, was practice.

—Jack Nicklaus, *Golf Digest*, 1991

212

You can be the greatest iron player in the world or the greatest putter, but if you can't get the ball in position to use your greatness, you can't win.

—Ben Hogan

There is no such thing as a natural touch. Touch is something you create by hitting millions of golf balls.

—Lee Trevino

They say 'practice makes perfect.' Of course, it doesn't. For the vast majority of golfers it merely consolidates imperfection.

—Henry Longhurst

To play winning golf, you have to have your personal life in order so that you can be focused on the course.

—Fuzzy Zoeller, from *Grip It and Rip It* by John Daly and John Andrisani

Make the basic shot-making decision early, clearly, and firmly, and then ritualize all the necessary acts of preparation.

—Sam Snead

Confidence is the most important single factor in this game, and no matter how great your natural talent, there is only one way to obtain and sustain it: work.

—Jack Nicklaus

But golf is fluid. It's always evolving, changing, you are never there. That's the beauty of it—waking up tomorrow trying to become a better player. I enjoy that.

—Tiger Woods

I realized that achieving my goal of being number one was not a matter of improving my swing; it was about me improving as a total player—and as a person. Every shot must have a purpose.

—Annika Sörenstam

No golfer can ever become too good to practice.

—May Hezlet

215

I want to win every week. I go to the driving range and bop 'til I drop.

—Rocky Thompson

Go find some stimulating, fulfilling, challenging human endeavor that, unlike golf, does not require a commitment of time and effort to realize maximum enjoyment. And call me when you find it.

—Jim Flick

CHAPTER 12

STARDOM

I'll sign everything. But please don't shove stuff at me, especially pens. I ruin about three hundred and sixty-five shirts a year from pens.
—Arnold Palmer

Arnold [Palmer] said to the waitress: 'You shouldn't use this kind of ketchup; Heinz is better.' After she left, I asked him: 'What's with the ketchup?' He said: 'I have a ketchup contract.'
—Ray Cave

It's hard being the father of a famous son.
—Jack Nicklaus, after Jack Nicklaus II won an amateur tournament.

I asked my wife, Gill, if she wanted a Versace dress, diamonds, or pearls as a present and she said no. When I asked her what she did want, she said: 'A divorce,' but I told her I wasn't planning to spend that much.

—Nick Faldo

Somebody asked me once, Who's better? Jack Nicklaus or Ben Hogan? Well, my answer was, I saw Nicklaus watch Hogan practice. But I never saw Hogan watch Nicklaus.

—Tommy Bolt

I don't like to be honored by anything. I don't see why anybody makes a big deal out of a poor little Mexican guy that hits a golf ball better than most people.

—Lee Trevino

I never wanted to be a millionaire. I just wanted to live like one.

—Walter Hagen

All you got to do to write a book is win one tournament. All of a sudden, you're telling everybody where the Vs ought to point. And them that don't win, they're haberdashers. They sell sweaters and slacks and call themselves pros.

—George Low

Nowadays, wherever I go, people say, 'That's the man who got the double eagle.' Actually, it was just a piece of luck. They forget the championships I won.

—Gene Sarazen

I opened my locker and there were a dozen new shirts, boxes of balls and two pairs of golf shoes. Now that I can afford them, they give them to me.

—Paul Azinger

I did envisage being this successful as a player, but not all the hysteria around it off the golf course.

—Tiger Woods

I played the Tour in 1967 and told jokes and nobody laughed. Then I won the Open the next year, told the same jokes, and everybody laughed like hell.

—Lee Trevino

I just love American girls. That is a big attraction for me over here. The girls have class and are incredibly beautiful. There are nice girls in Europe, but not too many of them get to golf events.

—Sergio Garcia

What I want is to be obscure and happy.

—Ian Baker-Finch

Playing golf is not hot work. Cutting sugar cane for a dollar a day—that's hot work. Hotter than my first wrist watch.

—Chi-Chi Rodriguez

223

I learned you can't drink whiskey and play golf.
—John Daly

I don't like the glamour. I just like the game.
—Ben Hogan

The players themselves can be classified into two groups—the attractions and the entry fees.
—Jimmy Demaret

Someday I'll tell my grandkids I played in the same tournament as Tiger Woods. We are witnessing a phenomenon here that the game may never, ever see again.
—Tom Watson

I suspect that the Jones humor has been what
really got him through all those years of being
a celebrity in our country.

—Paul Gallico

A big-name winner like Palmer is a modern
King Midas. Everything he drinks, smokes,
wears, or drives can turn to gold. All he has to
do is testify, yes, that's what I put on my hair,
smoke, drink, wear, drive, swing and hit.

—Tony Lema

God said to Faldo, as He once said to Nicklaus: 'You will have the skills like no other.' Then he whispered to Ballesteros, as he whispered to Palmer, 'But they will love you more.'

—Tom Callahan

You can make a lot of money in this game. Just ask my ex-wives. Both of them are so rich that neither of their husbands work.

—Lee Trevino

To be truthful, I think golfers are overpaid. It's unreal, and I have trouble dealing with the guilt sometimes.

—Colin Montgomerie

More people show up to watch Lee Trevino change shoes than watch me tee off.

—Orville Moody

Showmanship was needed and happily I possessed a flair for that, too, and I used it. In fact some fellows sort of believed I invented the kind of showmanship which, in those early days, began to put golf on a big-time money basis.

—Walter Hagen

I don't answer the phone. I get the feeling whenever I do that there will be someone on the other end.

—Fred Couples

I got my name in the record books and for every golf ball I hit I got to know someone . . . caddies, kings, golf fans, and even a few phonies.

—Walter Hagen

Nobody cares if John Daly shoots 80. They just want to see him hit a ball.

—Gene Sarazen

How long does John Daly drive a golf ball? When I was a kid, I didn't go that far on vacation.

—Chi-Chi Rodriguez

CHAPTER 13

COURSES

Golf architecture is the art and science of designing and building golf courses, and it involves much knowledge of landscape, soils, grasses, water, drainage, engineering, and sometimes—I feel—black magic.
   —Alistair Cooke, *Workers, Arise! Shout Fore*

There's no such thing as a green with too much slope.

—Tom Doak

If you try to fight the course, it will beat you.

—Lou Graham

230

The ardent golfer would play Mount Everest if somebody put a flagstick on top.

—Pete Dye

Would you like to see a city given over soul and body to a tyrannizing game? If you would, there's little need to rove, for St. Andrews is the abject city's name.

—R.F. Murray, 1885

St. Andrews? I feel like I'm back visiting an old grandmother. She's crotchety and eccentric but also elegant. Anyone who doesn't fall in love with her has no imagination.

—Tony Lema

Game plan? St. Andrews is the only course in the world where the only thing you try to do is miss all the bunkers. That's the game plan.

—Steve Elkington

There's nothing wrong with the Old Course at St. Andrews that a hundred bulldozers couldn't put right.

—Ed Furgol

The worst piece of mess I've ever played. I think they had some sheep and goats there that died and they just covered them up.

—Scott Hoch, after playing the Old Course at St. Andrews

Until you play it, St. Andrews looks like the sort of real estate you couldn't give away.

—Sam Snead

You know you're in for a challenge when the rough comes up over your shoes.

—Ernie Els, *Golf Digest*

Good greens have done nothing but give the golfer a split personality. First, he is a violent, physical athlete who tries to slash enormous divots out of the fairways . . . But when on the green, the golfer becomes . . . a solemn, timid, prayerful soul who wants only to peck tenderly at the ball.

—Dan Jenkins

I think I'll go cold turkey in the end and build golf courses. I'll torture other people.

—David Feherty

The trick for the developer, as devised through his architect, is to build something that is photogenically stunning, however impractical, extravagant or absurd. Never mind the golfer, that most gullible of all citizens.

—Peter Thomson

Golf architects can't play golf themselves and make damn sure that no one else can.

—Anonymous

Courses

When the ducks are walking, you know it is too windy to be playing golf.

—Dave Stockton

A ball will always come to rest halfway down a hill, unless there is sand or water at the bottom.

—Henry Beard

Golf is not a fair game, so why build a course fair?

—Pete Dye

I like going there for golf. America's one vast golf course these days.

—Edward VIII, Duke of Windsor

This is another thing I like about golf, the exclusiveness. Of course most country clubs exclude the wrong kinds of people, such as me. But I hold out the hope that somewhere there's a club that bans first wives.

—P.J. O'Rourke

No other game combines the wonder of nature with the discipline of sport in such carefully planned ways. A great golf course both frees and challenges a golfer's mind.

—Tom Watson

I just do not want to play these long, dull, wide-open turf nursery courses any more. Where is the challenge in just beating at the ball? Length is only one factor.

—Jack Nicklaus

Great golf courses seem to have an uncanny way of producing wonderful golf tournaments, with unforgettable shots and world-class champions.

—Gary Player, *Top Golf Courses of the World*

Bunkers have long been steeped in mystique and the best of them are the stuff of legend.

—Derek Lawrenson,
*Step-By-Step Golf Techniques:
Mastering the Long and Short Game*

237

The behavior etiquette for greenside bunkers should go into reverse. Players should be forbidden to smooth them in any way. The bunker should be the fearful place it once was, not the perfect surface from which a pro expects to float his ball out stone dead.

—Michael Halls

The object of the bunker or trap is not only to punish a physical mistake, to punish a lack of control, but also to punish pride and egotism.

—Charles Blair Macdonald

If some hole does not possess striking individuality through some gift of nature, it must be given as much as possible artificially, and the artifice must be introduced in so subtle a manner as to make it seem natural.

—A.W. Tillinghast

A golf course is the epitome of all that is purely transitory in the universe, a space not to dwell in, but to get over as quickly as possible.

—Jean Giraudoux

Always count your blessings. Be thankful you are able to be out on a beautiful course. Most people in the world don't have that opportunity.

—Fred Couples

Palm Springs is an inland sandbar man has wrested from rodents and the Indians to provide a day camp for over-privileged adults.
—Jim Murray

A golf course is an outdoor insane asylum peopled with madmen suffering from the delusion that they will finally master the game.
—Robert H. Davis

Golfers love punishment. And that's where I come in.
—Pete Dye, golf course architect

The object of inventors is to reduce the skill required for golf. If it were not for the counterskill of architects, the game would be emasculated.

—John L. Low, a founder of the Oxford and Cambridge golfing society in 1897

Water holes are sacrificial waters where you make a steady gift of your pride and high-priced golf balls.

—Tommy Bolt

Dream golf is simply golf played on another course. We chip from glass tables onto moving stairways; we swing in a straitjacket, through masses of cobweb, and awaken not with any sense of unjust hazard but only with a regret that the round can never be completed.

—John Updike

Golf courses are not the countryside—they're outdoors for people who wish the countryside had wiped clean surfaces.

—Linda Smith

To learn golf architecture one must know golf itself, its championship, its joys, its sorrows, its battles—one must play golf and love it.
—George Thomas, golf course architect

A good golf course is like good music. It does not necessarily appeal the first time one plays it.
—Alister Mackenzie

A golf course is nothing but a poolroom moved outdoors.
—Barry Fitzgerald

Bunkers are not placed on a course haphazard, but they are made at particular places to catch particular kinds of defective shots.

—James Braid

Golf courses are like children. I have no favorite.

—Robert Trent Jones, Sr.

Every hole should be a difficult par and a comfortable bogey.

—Robert Trent Jones

The more you study the course, the more you appreciate what a great test it is.

—Phil Mickelson

I think Darth Vader is actually a USGA official.
—Johnny Miller, on the course preparations
for major championships

Golf courses are beautiful. Many people think
mature men have no appreciation for beauty
except in immature women. That isn't true, and
anyway, we'd rather be playing golf.
—P.J. O'Rourke

Anyone who criticizes a golf course is like a
person invited to a house for dinner who, on
leaving, tells the host that the food was lousy.
—Gary Player

CHAPTER 14

THE FUTURE OF GOLF

I used to go to the bar when I finished a round. The kids today go back and practice.

—Lee Trevino

In thirty years, we're going to be in our nineties. We're going to play three-hole tournaments for $900,000 and the one who remembers his score wins.

—Bob Bruce, Senior PGA Tour member

In playing golf for more than fifty years, I don't believe there ever was a round in which I used more than six clubs . . . Today there's a stick in the sack for every shot . . . Golfers used to be made on the golf course. Now they are made in the machine shops.

—Donald Ross

That's what we need, some guys that have done well at their level. I tell them they're far more advanced at their age than I was. I couldn't play like they could when I was in my early twenties.

—Mike Weir

I'm not smart enough to figure out if it's good for the game or not.
—Fred Couples, on the proposed World Tour

I think it is wrong. I think the idea of paying players to play or reducing the field is ludicrous. I think when you start paying players and reducing fields that is the beginning of the end.
—Peter Jacobsen

Golf twenty years from now will continue to be the most civil of all popular competitive sports. There will be no trash talking, no attempts to circumvent rules, no physical threatening of competitors, no arguing with officials. For those reasons alone we can be proud as we look ahead.

—Gary Wiren, from "I Told You So: Two decades after his predictions for 2001 came true, our swami forecasts where golf is headed in the next twenty years," *Golf Digest*

The Future of Golf

How do they learn to play? Courses are so
busy and many of them are restrictive for kids.
I worry about this.
—Bill Ogden, ex-club professional, North Shore
Country Club, on kids not being allowed to play
at country clubs

The best thing we can do is fifty years
from now look back on our lives and say:
'We're good fathers.' I don't care how many
tournaments we win and how much money we
make. If we aren't a good dad, we leave the
world a bad place.

—Brad Bryant

CHAPTER 15

IMPACT OF GOLF

There are now more golf clubs in the world than Gideon Bibles, more golf balls than missionaries, and, if every golfer in the world, male and female, were laid end to end, I, for one, would leave them there.

—Michael Parkinson,
President of the anti-golf society

The best thing about Eisenhower's presidency was his Jeffersonian conviction that there should be as little government and as much golf as possible.

—Alistair Cooke

You can, legally, possibly hit and kill a fellow golfer with a ball, and there will not be a lot of trouble because the other golfers will refuse to stop and be witnesses because they will want to keep playing.

—Dave Barry

I don't consider myself a great black hope. I'm just a golfer who happens to be black and Asian.

—Tiger Woods

A lot of kids watch football and basketball, and that's fine . . . If they don't see any other African-Americans playing golf, then you don't want to do it, either.

—Jim Dent

Involving minorities in the game of golf has financial, political, and social implications. But the bottom line is simple: the more people who play the game, the fewer problems we'll have in the world. Because the game itself teaches people so much about themselves and others.

—Earl Woods

Cheap golf, it is accepted, is the Scotsman's birthright.

—Peter Dobereiner

Only in America can you explain a man working three days and making $52,000.

—Chi-Chi Rodriguez

The Englishman is at his best on the links and at his worst in the Cabinet.

—George Bernard Shaw

If you think about it, the golf ball doesn't know what country you're in.

—Annika Sörenstam

256

I remember [country singer] Charlie Pride and he said: 'Always pass the buck down. Don't keep it all in your pocket' . . . For us golfers, our main focus is giving.

—Jim Dent

It all comes back to the all-exempt Tour. It ruined the game . . . If you miss a cut and have to qualify to play next week, it's a whole different ball game. Half of them making more than $100,000 a year would be back home.

—Bob Drum

As you walk down the fairway of life, you must smell the roses, for you only get to play one round.

—Ben Hogan

Golf's reliance and regard for personal responsibility also outdistances other sports; perhaps that carries over off the course.

—Jim Apfelbaum

It is not a matter of life and death. It is not that important. But it is a reflection of life, and so the game is an enigma wrapped in a mystery impaled on a conundrum.

—Peter Alliss

Men trifle with their business and their politics but never trifle with their games. It brings truth home to them. They cannot pretend they have won when they have lost nor that they have had a magnificent drive when they have foozled it.

—George Bernard Shaw

One of the most fascinating things about golf is how it reflects the cycle of life. No matter what you shoot, the next day you have to go back to the first tee and begin all over again and make yourself into something.

—Peter Jacobsen

259

And the wind shall say: Here were decent godless people. Their only monument the asphalt road. And a thousand lost golf balls.

—T.S. Eliot

I would like to think of myself as an athlete first, but I don't want to do a disservice to the real ones.

—David Duval

Golf is used by people of every color, race, creed, and temperament, in every climate. No recreation, apart from the simple contests of the river and field, has been so universal since the world began.

—Henry Leach

The pat on the back, the arm around the
shoulder, the praise for what was done right
and the sympathetic nod for what wasn't are
as much a part of golf as life itself.
—President Gerald Ford

CHAPTER 16

GOLF JOKES

A couple has played golf every day for fifty years. One day the wife says, "Honey, to celebrate five decades of golf and marriage, let's start off with a clean slate and confess all our past wrongs."

"Okay," the husband says. "Do you remember that blond secretary who worked for me twenty years ago? Well, I had an affair with her."

And the wife says, "That's nothing. Before we met, I had a sex change."

And the husband says, "Why, you dang cheat! All this time you've been hitting from the red tees!"

—Willie Nelson

Golfer: The doctor says I can't play golf.

Caddie: Oh, he's played with you, too, huh?
                                    —Anonymous

I don't want to say Colin Montgomerie and Darren Clarke are big, but if you took a picture of them together from behind, it would look like one of these double greens.
                                    —Steve Elkington

Let's see, I think right now I'm third in money-winning and first in money-spending.
                                    —Tony Lema

I'd move heaven and earth to be able to break 100 on this course," sighed Mac the golfer.

"Try heaven," advised the caddie. "You've already moved most of the earth."
                                        —Anonymous

"That can't be my ball, caddie. It looks far too old," said the player, looking at a ball deep in the trees. The caddie replied, "It's a long time since we started, sir."
                                        —Anonymous

A golfer hits a huge slice off the first tee. The ball soars over a fence and onto a highway, where it hits a car, which promptly crashes into a tree.

The stunned golfer rushes into the golf shop and shouts, "Help! Help! I just hit a terrible slice off the first tee and hit a car and it crashed. What should I do?"

And the pro says, "Try a slightly stronger grip."

—Anonymous

A group of golfers were putting on the green when suddenly a ball dropped in their midst.

One of the party winked at the others and kicked the ball in the hole. Seconds later, a very fat player puffed on to the green quite out of breath and red of face.

He looked round distractedly and asked: "Seen my ball?"

"Yeah, it went in the hole," the joker answered with a straight face. The fat one looked at him unbelievingly. Then he walked to the hole, looked in, reached down and picked up his ball. His astonishment was plain to see. Then he turned, ran down the fairway and as he neared

267

his partner the group on the green heard him shout: "Hey, Sam, I got an eleven."

—Anonymous

He could do mankind a wonderful service, I suggested, if he signed into law the death penalty for slow-playing golfers.

—Dan Jenkins, on President George H. Bush, *Golf with the Boss*

A hack golfer spends a day at a plush country club, playing golf and enjoying the luxury of a complimentary caddie. Being a hack golfer, he plays poorly all day. Round about the 18th hole, he spots a lake off to the left of the fairway. He looks at the caddie and says, "I've played so poorly all day, I think I'm going to go drown myself in that lake."

The caddy looks back at him and says, "I don't think you could keep your head down that long."

—Anonymous

Lee Trevino doesn't want to talk about his back operation. That's all behind him.

—Don Criqui

Ever since my wife found it in the glove compartment.

—Lee Trevino, asked when he started wearing a corset for his bad back

A married man was having an affair with his secretary. One day, their passions overcame them and they took off for her house, where they made passionate love all afternoon. Exhausted from wild sex, they fell asleep and awoke at around 8 p.m. As the man threw on his clothes, he told the woman to take his shoes outside and rub them through the grass and dirt. Mystified, she nonetheless complied and he slipped into his shoes and drove home.

"Where have you been?" demanded his wife when he entered the house.

"Darling," replied the man, "I can't lie to you.
I've been having an affair with my secretary
and we've been having sex all afternoon. I fell
asleep and didn't wake up until eight o'clock."

The wife glanced down at his shoes and said,
"You lying bastard! You've been playing golf!"
—Anonymous

After a series of disastrous holes, the strictly
amateur golfer in an effort to smother his rage
laughed hollowly and said to his caddie:

"This golf is a funny game."

"It's not supposed to be," said the caddie
gravely.
—Anonymous

272

After coming from a long round of golf, his wife kissed her husband and kissed their son who came in a few moments later.

"Where's he been?" the husband asked.

"He's been caddieing for you all afternoon," the wife replied.

"No wonder he looks so familiar!"

—Anonymous

Golfer: Caddiemaster, that boy isn't even eight years old.

Caddiemaster: Better that way, sir. He probably can't count past ten.

—Anonymous

Golfer: Do you think I can get there with a 5-iron?

Caddie: Eventually.

—Anonymous

A wife asks her husband, "If I were to die, would you get married again and share our bed with your new wife?"

He responds, " I guess I might."

"What about my car?" she asks. "Would you give that to her?"

He says, "Perhaps."

"Would you give my golf clubs to her, too?" his wife asks.

"No."

"Why not?" asks the wife.

"She's left-handed."

—George Archer

Golfer: Notice any improvement today, Jimmy?

Caddie: Yes, ma'am. You've had your hair done.

—Anonymous

Golfer: This is the worst golf course I've ever played on!

Caddie: This isn't the golf course, sir! We left that an hour ago!

—Anonymous

Golfer: Well Caddie, how do you like my game?

Caddie: Very good, sir! But personally I prefer golf.

—Anonymous

Golfer: Caddie, do you think it is a sin to play golf on Sunday?

Caddie: The way you play, sir, it's a crime any day of the week.

—Anonymous

Golfer: Caddie, do you think my game is improving?

Caddie: Oh yes, sir! You miss the ball much closer than you used to.

—Anonymous

Golfer: Please stop checking your watch all the time, caddie. It's distracting!

Caddie: This isn't a watch, sir, it's a compass!

—Anonymous

Golfer: Caddie, why didn't you see where the ball went?

Caddie: Well, it doesn't usually go anywhere, Mr. Smith. You caught me off guard.

—Anonymous

Golfer: Well, I have never played this badly before!

Caddie: I didn't realize you had played before, sir.

—Anonymous

On the phone with a golf buddy who has asked him to play, a guy says: "I am the master of my home and can play golf whenever I want. But hold on a minute while I find out if I want to."

—Anonymous

CHAPTER 17

MAJOR TOURNAMENTS: FROM THE MASTERS TO THE RYDER CUP

Every kid learning to play golf dreams about winning the Masters, and about winning the Open, not about being the leading money winner.

—Tom Kite

I held the putter in a vice-like grip and from the moment I took it back from the ball I was blind and unconscious.

—Tommy Armour, on how he holed the putt that won him the 1931 Open Championship

I kept getting tears in my eyes. It happened to me once at Baltusrol. But here, it happened to me four or five times. I had to say to myself, Hey, you've got some golf to play.

—Jack Nicklaus, on the 1986 Masters

I used to think you could win just a bunch of other tournaments, but, well, I never would have said it, but I guess you have to win Majors to be up there. The longer you play, the more you realize that they are more important.

—Andy Bean

A major golf tournament is 40,000 sadists watching 144 masochists.

—Thomas Boswell

The finishes of the Masters Tournament have almost always been dramatic and exciting. It is my conviction that this has been because of the make-or-break quality of the second nine.

—Robert Trent Jones, Sr.

It's tough to see a grown man beg—unless it's a US Open winner momentarily letting down his guard and entreating the mercy of the golf gods.

—Jim Apfelbaum

At my age I've got to think positively. I'm 43
next week, and it's nice I can come back to
this tournament and do well again, and I look
forward to coming back here again next year
and trying another U.S. Open disaster.
                                    —Colin Montgomerie

I don't play great golf a lot. I do it every now
and then like in the British Open last year when
I finished third so I know I can do it . . . It's just
a matter of going out there and doing it again.
                                    —Fred Couples

When I'm through, I'll really miss kicking myself to get it done. I can live without playing the Masters. But the really satisfying time is the three weeks leading up to the Masters when I'm preparing for it.

—Jack Nicklaus

I'm a big believer in fate . . . I have a good feeling about this.

—Ben Crenshaw, the night before his American team overcame a four-point deficit to beat Europe at the Ryder Cup

If I knew what was going through Jack Nicklaus's head, I would have won this golf tournament.

—Tom Weiskopf

You've got a fairly good idea as to what the questions are going to be. But how to record the best answer is another matter.

—Nick Faldo, equating the U.S. Open to an exam

At its worst, the Open eradicates the difference in ability between a Tom Purtzer and a Tom Watson and throws both in the same jail of high rough and high risk shots. . . .

—Thomas Boswell

If I could just putt, I might just scare
somebody. Maybe me.

—Jack Nicklaus

Of the big four, the PGA is the most fair and
the least fun. Basically, it's just the US Open
set up by nice, rather than nasty, fellows.

—Thomas Boswell

I've got no business going to the U.S. Open
this week and playing a hard course like
Medinah.

—Lou Graham, before his victory
at the 1975 U.S. Open

If I can't play this last nine in thirty-seven strokes, I'm just a bum and don't deserve to win the Open.

—Ralph Guldahl, at the turn before winning the 1937 U.S. Open

Bobby [Jones] was playing some good golf in spots. He's got everything he needs to win any championship, except experience and maybe philosophy. But I'll tip you off to something. Bobby will win an Open before he wins an Amateur.

—Walter Hagen (Jones won the 1923 U.S. Open as his first Major title)

The British Open probably would have died if the American stars hadn't started going over to play in it more regularly the last fifteen years. Arnold Palmer saved it, but as far as I'm concerned he didn't do us any favours.

—Dave Hill

For an amateur, standing on the first hole of the Masters is the ultimate laxative.

—Trevor Homer

You start to choke at the Masters when you drive through the front gate.

—Hale Irwin

I looked up and there was a streaker on the course, running back and forth on the green, dodging the cops. When he turned and ran toward me, I just nailed him—I did my great Jack Lambert imitation.

—Peter Jacobsen, on tackling a streaker at the 1985 British Open

It's the old American thing from the Ryder Cup matches. The Americans wear Foot-joys and all the English players stand together admiring their shoes and their slacks and their clubs. How can you beat a man if you can't afford his shoes?

—Nick Job

At Augusta National they bikini-wax the greens.
—Gary McCord, a comment that saw him banned from the Masters as a television commentator

The logic is that every sport ends with a bonanza, and ours doesn't. The Tour Championship is going up against football and the World Series. We need to stand on our own.

—Billy Andrade

Any time you save par out of the rough in this tournament, you feel like you've escaped from jail. It's like a get-out-of-jail-free-card.

—Tom Lehman, on the U.S. Open

By the time I got to the first tee in my first Masters, I was so scared I could hardly breathe. If you're not a little nervous there, there isn't anything in life that can make you nervous.

—Roger Maltbie

You just can't miss putts and win tournaments, whether it's the Atlanta Classic or the Masters.

—Fred Couples

If you're going to be a player people will remember, you have to win the Open at St. Andrews.

—Jack Nicklaus

Playing in the U.S. Open is like tippy-toeing through hell.

—Jerry McGee

The Ryder Cup is a hard face-to-face match, and because [players] are not used to that kind of confrontation, they feel the heat. And it shows.

—Johnny Miller, *Golf Digest*

Form goes out the window at the Ryder Cup. On the Friday morning, on the first tee, it's not how's your form but whether you can stand up.

—Colin Montgomerie

You don't come to Augusta to find your game.
You come here because you've got one.
—Gene Sarazen, on the Masters

I finally found the guy I used to know on the
golf course. It was me.
—Jack Nicklaus, after winning his
6th Masters in 1986

At its best, the U.S. Open demands straight
drives, crisp iron shots, brilliant chipping and
putting, and strategic position play. Plus the
patience of St. Francis and the will of Patton.
—Thomas Boswell

I think the great thing about the Ryder Cup is that the players are really playing for their countries and not playing for money. I think that is the important essence of the Ryder Cup.

—Bernard Gallagher

It's the only pure golf tournament we play in, including all of the other major championships. No skyboxes here or anything like that. You see the same faces in the gallery come tournament time. Over the years, I get to know the people and where they sit.

—Greg Norman, on the Masters

Nobody wins the [U.S.] Open. It wins you.
—Cary Middlecoff

In America, the Ryder Cup rates somewhere between the Tennessee Frog Jumping Contest and the Alabama Melon-Pip Spitting Championship, although the players themselves have always taken it seriously—until Tom Weiskopf declined to play in favor of a week's holiday shooting sheep.
—Peter Dobereiner

When the British Open is in Scotland, there's something special about it. And when it's at St. Andrews, it's even greater.
—Jack Nicklaus

The things I have seen in the Ryder Cup have disappointed me. You are hearing about hatred and war.

—Gary Player

If you like root canals and hemorrhoids, you'd love it there.

—Nick Price, on the Ryder Cup

The first time I played the Masters, I was so nervous I drank a bottle of rum before I teed off. I shot the happiest 83 of my life.

—Chi-Chi Rodriguez

We all say majors are just another 72-hole tournament. In a way, they are. But we're really just saying that to keep ourselves from getting too fired up.

—Curtis Strange

We're not trying to humiliate the worst players in the world . . . we're trying to identify them.

—Frank Tatum, USGA President,
on the selection of U.S. Open courses

If that's golf, I'm in the wrong damn league.

—Fuzzy Zoeller, complaining about the
conditions of the greens at the Masters

Hell, man, Ray Charles could play here . . . and it still wouldn't make no difference.

> —Lee Trevino, on the subtleties of Muirfield during the 1972 British Open

The last year's champion serves as the host. He chooses the menu and picks up the tab. When I discovered the cost of the dinner was more than the prize money, I finished second four times.

> —Ben Hogan, on the Masters dinner

There is absolutely nothing humorous at the Masters. Here, small dogs do not bark and babies do not cry.

> —Gary Player

My wife will find ways to spend $16,000 first-prize money in sixteen minutes.
—Julius Boros, on winning the 1963 U.S. Open

In other sports they don't do anything differently than they have done all year, but golf is the only game that changes for a major event.

—Raymond Floyd

I must admit the name was born of a touch of immodesty.
　　—Bobby Jones, the founder of the Masters

Leave all the social significance aside. This is like watching Babe Ruth in the 1920s.

> —George Will, on Tiger Woods winning the 1997 Masters

I want the Masters bad! I'm going to Augusta in April and eating crow on the front steps.

> —Lee Trevino, after years of criticizing the Masters

They talk about the majors and how important they are. But you're playing the same guys you play every week, just on another golf course.

> —Sam Snead

The USGA makes sure that every [U.S.] Open is a paramount test of a player's ability to use the game's most definitive clubs, the driver and the putter.

—Thomas Boswell

He's going to win more of these [Master's titles] than Arnold [Palmer] and I combined.

—Jack Nicklaus, after a practice round with Tiger Woods in 1996

There should never, ever be a sense of inevitability about golf. Too much can go wrong, especially in a major championship. One half-bad swing, one gust of wind, one silly club selection can unravel it all, can turn apparent victory in disaster.

—Michael Wilbon, *Washington Post*

How's my name going to fit on that thing?

—Mark Calcavecchia,
on winning the Claret Jug

Is winning the Open worth a million pounds? Well, it's worthwhile winning it—I would recommend it to anybody.

—Sandy Lyle

303

The majors are what golf's all about. The other ones you play for the prize money. These you play to get your name on a piece of silver.

—Nick Faldo

Maybe if I knock on the door enough, the door will open one day.

—Colin Montgomerie, on coming close to winning a major tournament

When I woke up Sunday morning at the Open and stepped outside and felt the wind and rain in my face, I knew I had an excellent chance to win if I just took my time and trusted myself.

—Tom Kite, on finally winning a major, the 1992 U.S. Open

I suggested that Ghezzi begin play and I would join him on the third hole conceding him wins on the first two . . . The kid was just mad enough to beat me on the first two holes anyway, then I began to play. I finally caught him and won.

—Walter Hagen, describing his victory in the 1940 PGA Championship after Vic Ghezzi suggested before the match that Hagen hurry it up

Golfing excellence goes hand in hand with alcohol, as many an Open and Amateur champion has shown.

—Henry Longhurst

Only Opens.
—Tom Watson, when asked if he collected
anything Scottish for luck

Throwing up on myself.
—Curtis Strange, on what he felt like doing
after losing the 1985 Masters

I hit every shot the way I dreamed about
today. But that's the strange thing about golf.
You don't have any control about what your
opponent does.
—Tom Kite, losing the
1986 Masters to Jack Nicklaus

This lie is tighter than an Italian tenor's trouser buttons.

—Ken Brown, commenting on the
2004 Open Championship

Were you in prison in 1984? Maybe you didn't get copies of the newspaper there?

—Lee Trevino, 1984 PGA winner, upon being told by a reporter during the 1986 US Open that he hadn't won a major in a long time

I played 36 holes today with a kid who should have won this Open by ten shots.

—Ben Hogan, on the amateur
Jack Nicklaus at the 1960 US Open

I was so nervous today I was almost jumping out of my skin all day. Usually when I'm playing decent, I'm nervous.
—Tom Watson, on winning the 1981 Masters

A million thoughts went through my mind. What a little mind I have.
—Fuzzy Zoeller, after winning the Masters

CHAPTER 18

A PASSION FOR GOLF: WHY WE LOVE THIS GAME

If they don't have golf in heaven then I'm not going.

> —An inscription on a pillow in
> Arnold Palmer's home

I play because I like it, very much. I play golf for money when I play an exhibition. But when I play in a tournament I'm there because I enjoy it.

> —Seve Ballesteros

The amateur has an infectious, contagious enthusiasm for golf and life.

> —Mac O'Grady

310

Man blames fate for other accidents but feels personally responsible for a hole in one.
—Martha Beckman

How can you get tired of playing golf?
—-Raymond Floyd

I live for the loud smacking sound I hear when the clubface comes into the ball at high speed and contacts its center back portion, hard.
—John Daly, from *Grip It and Rip It* by John Daly and John Andrisani

I love golf but I'm not going to sacrifice everything for the game. If some people want to, I think it's wonderful.

—Gloria Armstrong

It's not a big risk to me . . . My sites are really so well-located, in such great areas, that if the golf were to fail, I could probably make more money putting housing on them. But I won't do that. I enjoy golf too much.

—Donald Trump

Woods and Kite play golf because they love it. To them it is art. They paint pictures with their clubs. Neither one can wait for the next day of golf.

—Jim McLean, from *The Eight-Step Swing*

What other people may find in poetry or art museums, I find in the flight of a good drive.

—Arnold Palmer

I can only tell you one thing that I do know for sure, I am a dreamer . . . I continue to get up in the morning, enthusiastically, and go pick up a golf club with a thought that I can somewhere find that secret to making the cut.

—Arnold Palmer

Golf may be a hussy, but I love her.

—Don Herold

The great thing about golf—and this is the reason why a lot of health experts like me recommend it—you can drink beer and ride in a cart while you play.

—Dave Barry

Golf to me is not a business; it's an art form, like a Picasso or a Steinbeck novel.

—Tom Watson

The fun you get from golf is in direct ratio to the effort you don't put into it.

—Bob Allen

Golf may be . . . a sophisticated game. At least, it is usually played with the outward appearance of dignity. It is, nevertheless, a game of considerable passion, either of the explosive type, or that which burns inwardly and sears the soul.

—Bobby Jones

When you fall in love with golf, you seldom fall easy. It's obsession at first sight.

—Thomas Boswell

I like it for the same reason a lot of other busy people don't: I like it because it takes so much time.

—President Bill Clinton

Just having fun. Got to do it while I've still got it.

—Tiger Woods

This game is great and very strange.

—Seve Ballesteros

I love golf. It is a wonderful game, one that at any given moment, with any given shot, you can do as well as the best player in the world.

—Bob Costas

I try to play every day and when I don't play—if you'll excuse the expression—I feel like a bear with a sore tail because of it.

—Arnold Palmer

This is the best. This is just too perfect, so serene, so peaceful. There's nothing like it.

—Ben Crenshaw

I just love to play golf. I try to play 365 days a year. I don't care if it's January or June. I wanted to play on Christmas Day, but my wife looked at me kind of funny, so I thought I'd better not.

—Lee Trevino

Love is the ultimate outlaw. It just won't adhere to any rules. The most any of us can do is sign on as its accomplice.

—Tom Watson, on golf

Golf is more than a mere game. It is a religion.

—Walter Travis

I feel very fortunate to make a living playing a game I love and look forward to the next ten years.

—Tiger Woods

The simple truth is I love Scottish golf and all the peculiar experience that embraces.

—James Dodson

Golf obviously provides one of our best forms of healthful exercise accompanied by good fellowship and companionship.

—President Dwight D. Eisenhower

I'm just playing for the love of the game. And for the little cups.

—Nick Faldo

I don't like going to the mall. I'm not really like the other girls. I just like to go out on the golf course and play. Golf is fun and feels really good.

—Michelle Wie

I play golf so I can fly. At $2 a gallon for fuel, I have to support my habit somehow.

—Bill Glasson

I owe everything to golf. Where else would a guy with an IQ like mine make this much money?

—Hubert Green

The game lends itself to fantasies about our abilities.

—Peter Alliss

After all, as every golfer in every land will attest after a good round, it may well be the best game ever invented.

—Herbert Warren Wind

Golf is just so much fun. I don't see how anybody can't have a great time out here doing what we're doing.

—Peter Jacobsen

There is a basic fascination with golf unlike other games. No ordinary person could go one round with the heavyweight boxing champion . . . But a golfer may at any time hit that one spectacular shot just as well as Ben Hogan, Arnold Palmer, or Greg Norman.

—Pete Dye

A tolerable day, a tolerable green, a tolerable opponent supply, or ought to supply, all that any reasonably constituted human should require in the way of entertainment.

—Arthur James

Regardless of what the Tour pros think, golf is a rich and varied game, and what all of us awkward fools do on weekends is what golf is truly all about.

—Dan Jenkins

I'm a golfaholic, no question about it. Counseling wouldn't help me. They'd have to put me in prison. And then I'd talk the warden into building a hole or two to teach him how to play.

—Lee Trevino

The great thing about this game is that the bad days are wonderful.

—President Bill Clinton

Unlike the other Scotch game of whisky-drinking, excess is not injurious to the health.
—Sir Walter Simpson

When I get out on that green carpet called a fairway, manage to poke the ball right down the middle, my surroundings look like a touch of heaven on earth.
—Jimmy Demaret

Golf charms by its infinite variety.
—Theodore Moone

Golf is deceptively simple and endlessly complicated; it satisfies the soul and frustrates the intellect. It is at the same time rewarding and maddening—and it is without a doubt the greatest game mankind has ever invented.

—Arnold Palmer

No round ever will be so good it could not have been better. Perhaps this is why golf is the greatest of games. You are not playing a human adversary; you are playing a game. You are playing old man par.

—Bobby Jones

Golf is the most fun you can have without taking your clothes off.

—Chi-Chi Rodriguez

The beauty of golf, you're in charge out here.

—Mike Weir

My only fear is that I may have to go out and get a real job.

—Fuzzy Zoeller

I like golf because I can go out and hit a little white ball that doesn't move and doesn't hit back. It should be easy, but it isn't.

—Lawrence Taylor

Golf will grow so long as it's fun.

—Tom Watson

That's my business [real estate], you understand? This golf thing isn't my business. I love it, but I'll make more money from selling A-Rod a place than I'd make all year from a golf course. But I get a kick out of the golf thing.

—Donald Trump

Golf appeals to the idiot in us and the child. Just how childlike golf players become is proven by their frequent inability to count past five.

—John Updike

327

I think at that time I really fell in love with the game. I'd always loved golf, but now it was a new type of love that I could have.

—Tom Watson, after beating Jack Nicklaus by one stroke in the 1977 British Open

I like golf cause—well, I reckon I jes' love to play the game.

—Sam Snead

Go out and have fun. Golf is a game for everyone, not just for the talented few.

—Harvey Penick

What is love compared with holing out before your opponent.

—P.G. Wodehouse

Golf to me isn't just something to do. I love this game. It's like a drug I have to have.

—Tiger Woods

I'm a guy who'll play with amateurs. A $50 Nassau, $500, $5,000 or nothing. It doesn't matter. I just like to play.

—Lee Trevino

I've never been to Heaven, and thinkin' back on my life, I probably won't get a chance to go. I guess the Masters is as close as I am going to get.

—Fuzzy Zoeller

There is no type of miracle that can't happen at least once in golf.

—Grantland Rice

Few things draw two men together more surely than a mutual inability to master golf, coupled with an intense and ever-increasing love for the game.

—P.G. Wodehouse

You can get close enough to mastering the game, to feel it, to breathe it, maybe to smell it. But you can't master it, not for a long time.

—Tom Watson

To dwell near a good course and work hard at the game; to go away whenever the spirit moved one . . . to some paradise by the seas with a pleasant companion or two; to stay as long as one liked . . . even to think of it is still to feel faintly the old desire.

—Bernard Darwin

It matters not the sacrifice which makes the duffer's wife sore. I am the captive of my slice, the servant of my score.

—Grantland Rice

You're only here for a short visit. Don't hurry, don't worry. And be sure to smell the flowers along the way.

—Walter Hagen

CHAPTER 19

CELEBRITIES ON THE LINKS: FROM MOVIE STARS TO PRESIDENTS

Finally I'm vindicated. I'm certainly one of the most talented athletes ever to come out of the Chicago area, and I've been largely unappreciated . . . but at least I'm able to claim the glory that is rightly mine . . . I am now recognized as a true athletic hero.

—Bill Murray, after defeating Michael Jordan and D.A. Weilbring in a charity event in Chicago

A fidgety player who addressed the ball as if he could reason with it.

—An anonymous characterization of President Woodrow Wilson's golf game

It took me seventeen years to get 3,000 hits in baseball. I did it in one afternoon on the golf course.

—Hank Aaron

I can't hit a ball more than 200 yards. I have no butt. You need a butt if you're going to hit a golf ball.

—Dennis Quaid

I played one of the days with Sam Jackson, George Lopez and Cheech Marin . . . Sam is over there contemplating the game of golf and what it means . . . and Cheech and George are trying to figure out who has had the best one-liner so far. That just cracks me up.

—Justin Leonard

When golf season comes around, I get like a piano player who doesn't shake hands with anybody for fear of hurting himself . . . I haven't reached an accommodation with that phobia, so here I sit, fat and soft.

—Bryant Gumbel

It's amazing how many people beat you at golf now that you're no longer president.

     —President George H. Bush

You can't do well if you're thinking about anything else . . . This is the nearest I ever am to being a normal person.

     —President Bill Clinton

The terrible beauty is that in the brotherhood of golf (feminists please excuse the term) we are all the same—certifiable.

     —Sean Connery

The problem with golf is I have to deal with a humiliation factor.

—President George H. Bush

It would have been like a friend of mine coming out of the stands to pass the time of day when I was at bat.
—Joe DiMaggio, when asked what he thought of talking to golfers while they were playing

Bob Hope's swing? I've seen better swings on a condemned playground.

—Bing Crosby

I'm a 16 at Sleepy Hollow, up in Westchester [NY]. Won one tournament there, and got a trophy—Headless Horseman. Figures. Best score ever: 79.

—Bill Murray

On one hole I'm like Arnold Palmer, and on the next like Lilli Palmer.

—Sean Connery

Lots of golfers spend their time wondering whether to lay up or go for it. I'm always going for it because that's the way I play football.

—Brett Favre

He has a good swing, he hits hard, a little erratic, but I understand that.
>—President Gerald Ford, on Bill Clinton

At least he can't cheat on his score because all you have to do is look back down the fairway and count the wounded.
>—Bob Hope, about Gerald Ford

I would like to deny all allegations by Bob Hope that during my last game of golf, I hit an eagle, a birdie, an elk and a moose.
>—President Gerald Ford

Give me my golf clubs, fresh air, and a
beautiful partner, and you can keep my golf
clubs and the fresh air.

—Jack Benny

That's Jack Benny. He's always out there on
bad days like that looking for golf balls.
—Bing Crosby, after a skin diver came out
of the water at the 16th hole of the
Crosby Pro-Am

Either he is an unbelievable athlete or I have a
career as a golf instructor.
—President Bill Clinton, to Prime Minister Tony
Blair after his first round of golf ever

Here Eddie, hold the flag while I putt out.
—Walter Hagen, to the Prince of Wales

You know, this is like having a Billy Martin in
your pocket.
—Mickey Mantle, on using a device
on the golf course that utters curses
at the push of a button

I think if I were going to pick three people I
could spend the day talking to, it would be
Lincoln and the two Roosevelts.
—President Bill Clinton

One lesson you better learn if you want to be in politics is that you never go out on a golf course and beat the President.

—President Lyndon Johnson

He hits the ball 130 yards and his jewelry goes 150.

—Bob Hope, on Sammy Davis Jr.

That looks like very good exercise. But what is the little white ball for?

—President Ulysses S. Grant

One time I was complaining that my shot
was going to wind up in the water. So my
friend Kevin Carroll told me that I should think
positive. I told him okay, I was positive my shot
was going to wind up in the water.

—Yogi Berra

I don't have any handicap. I am all handicap.

—President Lyndon Johnson

I can only thank Davis Love III for turning me
on to golf and showing me it isn't a sissy
game.

— Michael Jordan

I'll be playing center for the Bulls before
Michael [Jordan] plays on the tour.
                              —Peter Jacobsen

My golf is woeful but I will never surrender.
                              —Bing Crosby

Before I got out of the rough in one
tournament it had turned into a shopping
center.
                              —Bob Hope

Every time I look down, I think I'm in the
rough.
        —Jack Lemmon, on growing a moustache

A typical day in the life of a heavy metal musician consists of a round of golf and an AA meeting.

—Billy Joel

First of all, unless you're Charles Barkley, you have to have a low handicap. I don't want to go just to go—I want to have fun. I go to Pebble Beach to have fun, but I also think I can win. Did I just say that again?

—Bill Murray

I'd rather make the cut in the Crosby than win another Oscar.

—Jack Lemmon

I'd love to see John McEnroe join the PGA Tour, just so we could kick him out.

—Peter Jacobsen

Most of these guys only want to grow up and mature. When I retire, I'm going to enjoy being a black multi-millionaire.

—Charles Barkley, on the celebrity golf tour

I play in the low 80s. If it's any hotter than that, I won't play.

—Joe Louis

By the time you get dressed, drive out there, play 18 holes, and come home, you've blown seven hours. There are better things you can do with your time.

—President Richard Nixon

In golf, when we hit a foul ball, we got to go out and play it.

—Sam Snead, to baseball great Ted Williams

I would have been worried if they played well. It would have meant they were spending too much time playing golf and not enough time running the country.

—Seve Ballesteros, after playing with Portugal's President and Minister of Justice

I would rather play Hamlet with no rehearsal than play golf on television.

—Jack Lemmon

In golf, you keep your head down and follow through. In the vice presidency, you keep your head up and follow through. It's a big difference.

—Dan Quayle

There we go! Miles and miles and miles!
—Alan Shepard, after hitting a tee-shot on the moon

The Secret Service is in front of you. And the Air Force is flying over you. But the worst part is that the Marines are digging sand traps for your balls.

—Bob Hope, on playing with presidents

Swing hard in case you hit it.

—Dan Marino

He plays such a great game of golf for a guy wearing skis.

—Bob Hope, about President Gerald Ford

Got more dirt than ball. Here we go again.

—Alan Shepard, preparing to take another swing during his famous moon walk in 1971

If everybody in Washington in government service who belongs or has belonged to a restricted [golf] club was to leave government service, this city would have the highest rate of unemployment . . . in the country.

—President Richard Nixon

How about a little noise. How do you expect a man to putt?

—Babe Ruth

You've heard of Arnie's Army. Well, those are Dean's Drunks.

—Dean Martin, on his followers on the golf course

I've done as much for golf as Truman Capote
has done for sumo wrestling.

> —Bob Hope

Stick your butt out, Mr. President.

> —Sam Snead,
> advising President Eisenhower on his swing

President [George H.] Bush does not take
mulligans. That family plays by the rules.

> —Ben Crenshaw

Probably I'm a hell of a lot more famous for
being the guy who hit the golf ball on the
moon than the first guy in space.

> —Alan Shepard

I just can't find it when I hit it.

—Jerry West

The best part of this office is who you get to play golf with. I've played with Jack Nicklaus, Arnold Palmer, Raymond Floyd, Amy Alcott.

—President Bill Clinton

I was like, 'Oh my God, it's the secretary of state. They put me in charge of driving her around [in the golf cart].' I was like, 'If I crash, the secretary of state goes down with me.'

—Michelle Wie

Whenever I play with [President Ford], I usually try to make it a foursome—the president, myself, a paramedic, and a faith healer.

—Bob Hope

The best part is I've taken five strokes off my golf game.

—Ellen DeGeneres, on coming out of the closet

If Bill Clinton is an 8-handicap, I'm Bobby Jones.

—President George H. Bush

I may not know enough about being President, but I do know that a lot of decisions can be made on the golf course.

—President Warren Harding

Every time you swing you have a chance for greatness.

—Kevin Costner

I'm not feeling very well—I need a doctor immediately. Ring the nearest golf course.

—Groucho Marx

Hit till you're happy.

—President Lyndon Johnson

The greatest thrill of my life—even better than getting elected.

> —President Richard Nixon,
> on his first hole-in-one

I envy that man [golfer Miller Barber]. Because he makes a hundred thousand dollars a year like I do, but nobody knows him.

> —Mickey Mantle

Congress.

> —President Lyndon Johnson, when asked his handicap when he showed up at the Masters

It should be indulged in when the opportunity arises, as every man who has played the game knows that it rejuvenates and stretches the span of life.

—President William Howard Taft

If you drink, don't drive. Don't even putt.

—Dean Martin

Drugs are very much a part of professional sports today, but when you think about it, golf is the only sport where the players aren't penalized for being on grass.

—Bob Hope

I sold three memberships, at $350,000 apiece . . . at Trump International, just standing on the tee hitting golf balls. People walked up and gave me checks. I know that if I'm not there, those three people don't join . . . It's called the owner's touch. You have to have that personal touch.

—Donald Trump

The tour is a juggernaut. But there's a reason why people flock to see Sergio Garcia. Yeah, these guys are good. How about, these guys are good and fun?

—Bill Murray

The only time my prayers are never answered is on the golf course.

—Billy Graham

I'm a vice president in charge of special marketing. That means I play golf and go to cocktail parties. I'm pretty good at my job.

—Mickey Mantle

Obviously a deer on the fairway has seen you tee off before and knows that the safest place to be when you play is right down the middle.

—Jackie Gleason

I was hot. I was smoking 'em. Even a blind pig finds an acorn sometimes.
>—President Bill Clinton, on
>shooting his first 79

You have to let a little air into the war room now and then.
>—President Dwight D. Eisenhower,
>on enjoyment of golf

Don't ask what I shot.
>—President Dwight Eisenhower,

How has retirement affected my golf game? A lot more people beat me now.
>—President Dwight D. Eisenhower

I tried everything mental and physical I could
to help him out. After three or four holes, there
was nothing I could do. I ran out of ideas. I just
told him, 'I feel for you. I really do.'
 —Tom Watson, after being paired with NBA
 player Charles Barkley at a pro-am

My God, he looks like he's beating a chicken!
 —Byron Nelson, on actor Jack
 Lemmon's swing

Forget that I am president of the United
States. I am Warren Harding, playing with
some friends, and I'm going to beat the hell
out of them.

 —President Warren Harding

CHAPTER 20

LEGENDARY PLAYERS, LEGENDARY MOMENTS

I never played a round when I didn't learn something new about the game.

—Ben Hogan

I don't know very much. I know a little about golf. I know how to make a stew. And I know how to be a decent man.

—Byron Nelson

I'm glad we don't have to play in the shade.

—Bobby Jones, response to being told it was 105 degrees in the shade

People always ask me about one shot that won a tournament, and I really have trouble recalling a specific shot. But I will always remember that shot right there. I'll remember that putt because I don't know how it went in.

—Raymond Floyd

Seve Ballesteros and Greg Norman are the modern giants, the Michelangelos, the Picassos, the da Vincis. We are lucky we have them.

—Mac O'Grady

To me [Seve Ballesteros's] swing was perfect.

—Tom Weiskopf

To me, he's very boring. He's never in the trees or in the water. He's not the best driver, not the best putter. He's just the best at everything.

—Fred Couples, on Nick Faldo

Babe Zaharias was a remarkable person. She was no pantywaist, I'll tell you. She definitely was stronger than most men. When she walked, her muscles just rippled under her skin. She could hit longer than I could; so could Mickey Wright.

—Paul Runyon

In his most useful and tempestuous days he had never been angry and not often, I think with Fate, but he had been furiously angry with himself. He set himself an almost impossibly high standard . . . but he became outwardly a man of ice, with the very best of golfing manners.

—Bernard Darwin, on Bobby Jones

Jones: Mr. Vardon, did you ever see a worse shot than that?
Vardon: No.

——Harry Vardon, response to Bobby Jones when he skulled a niblick in the 1920 U.S. Open

A match against Bobby Jones is just as though you got your hand caught in a buzz saw. He coasts along serenely waiting for you to miss a shot, and the moment you do he has you on the hook and you never get off.

—Francis Ouimet

It is nonsense to talk about who was the greatest golfer in the world. All you can say is that there have been none greater than Bobby Jones.

—Tommy Armour

[Mure Ferguson] was a magnificent putter, standing straight up, noticeably far from the ball, and hitting it straight in. It really looked as if the ball knew better than to disobey him.

—Bernard Darwin

Ben Hogan would rather have a coral snake rolling inside his shirt than hit a hook.

—Claude Harmon

Tiger [Woods] is the dragon out there. Somebody had to slay him.

—Jeff Maggert

[Tiger Woods]'s playing a game I'm not familiar with. Of course, I'm playing a game I'm not familiar with.

—Jack Nicklaus

The only thing that can stop him is an injury or a bad marriage.

—Dan Jenkins, on Tiger Woods

I didn't want to be the bad guy. I wasn't trying to end the streak per se. I was just trying to win the golf tournament.

—Phil Mickelson, after beating Tiger Woods at the 2000 Buick Invitational

I don't know . . . I never played there.
>
> —Sandy Lyle, when asked
> what he thought of Tiger Woods

I would rather play a man who is straight down the fairway with his drive, on the green with his second, and down in two putts for his par. I can play a man like that at his own game, which is par golf.
>
> —Bobby Jones, after losing to
> Walter Hagen in match play in 1926

If it were not for you, Walter, this dinner would be downstairs in the pro shop and not in the ballroom.
>
> —Arnold Palmer, at a dinner in Hagen's honor

Walter broke 11 of the 10 Commandments.
—Fred Corcoran, on Walter Hagen

If this tour is a blood bank, he's going to be a Count Dracula having a gory feast.
—Gary McCord, on Tom Watson's Senior Tour debut

His control of the ball was such that he seemed to allow it no option but to go where he wanted it to go.
—Al Laney, on Ben Hogan

Actually, Ben didn't leave him himself much time for laughter. I can't recall him ever finding humor in anything that happened on the golf course. Golf was his business—a tough business, full of disappointments.

   —Fred Corcoran, on Ben Hogan

Put today's players against me in 1945, and I would have won more than six [tournaments]. I think I would have won nine tournaments. I was playing very well.

   —Byron Nelson, on his record-setting
    eighteen-victory campaign in 1945

So how did Nicklaus win so much? Because he could finish a hole better than anyone else. As a player he's the greatest of all time but as a golfer I can't even put him in the first fifty.

—"Wild" Bill Mehlhorn

It's hard not to play up to Jack Nicklaus's standards when you are Jack Nicklaus.

—Jack Nicklaus

When Jack Nicklaus plays well, he wins. When he plays badly, he finished second. When he plays terribly, he finished third.

—Johnny Miller

I would say with the technology we have today, with the equipment, if you put that in Jack Nicklaus's hands, he'd be a better golfer than Tiger Woods.

—Greg Norman

If I had to have someone putt a 20-footer for everything I own—my house, my cars, my family—I'd want Nicklaus to putt for me.

—Dave Hill

I've studied golf for almost fifty years now and know a hell of a lot about nothing.

—Gary Player

Michael Jordan strikes me as one of the greatest athletes who ever lived, but Sam Snead still goes down as the greatest. He's performed in his teens, his twenties, his thirties, his forties, his fifties, his sixties, and at seventy he finished second.

—Gary Player

[Walter] Hagen played in tournaments as though they were cocktail parties.

—Charles Price

When I'm through with my career, I'm going to look back and say, hey, I was part of this little chapter of my life of golf, for instance, but I'm enjoying that because I'm on top of all that. It's a great moment in my life, anyway.

—Vijay Singh

I saw him take one swing on the practice tee and I said that's the best golfer I'd ever seen . . . That's the first time I saw a spark fly when the club hit the ball.

—Gary Player, on the first time he saw Arnold Palmer swing a club

Never saw one who was worth a damn.

—Harry Vardon, describing left-handed golfers

377

Harry Vardon was a big man with huge hands. My own was practically lost in his hand shake. He was reserved, quiet, with almost nothing to say. But I learned plenty from watching him swing a golf club.

—Walter Hagen

Harry Vardon stands alone in all the glory that his performances testify.

—J.H. Taylor

Greg Norman looks like the guy they always hire to kill James Bond in the movies.

—Dan Jenkins

You know what we should have done? Taken Greg skiing.

— Brad Faxon, on Greg Norman easily winning the Tournament Players Championship after Mark Calcavecchia, Phil Mickelson, and Mark Weibe were all injured skiing

He is the most immeasurable of golf champions. But this is not entirely true because of all he has won, or because of that mysterious fury with which he has managed to rally himself. It is more than anything because of the pure unmixed joy he has brought back to trying.

— Dan Jenkins, on Arnold Palmer

379

On being asked how good Young Tom Morris really was, an aged golfer replied: 'I cannot imagine anyone playing better.'

—Anonymous

Walter Hagen was the greatest loser and greatest winner and the greatest golfer.

—Chick Evans

Hagen was the first professional to make a million dollars at the game—and the first to spend it.

—Fred Corcoran

Hidden under that famous straw hat of his is a
slick spot as wide as some fairways I've seen.
> —Tommy Bolt, on Sam Snead

The only reason I ever played golf in the first
place was so I could afford to hunt and fish.
> —Sam Snead

Arnold Palmer is an early riser. He is anxious
to get the day going because who knows how
many good things might happen.
> —Mary McCormack

CHAPTER 21

THE BACK NINE: ON THE SENIOR TOUR AND GETTING OLDER

I just hope I don't have to explain all the times
I've used His name in vain when I get up there.
                         —Bob Hope, on his golfing

If you drink, quit. If you smoke, cut down. That
covers the physical end of it. Then you've got
to get your brain in shape, which is even harder
to do and more important . . . Forget hitting
balls, it's lifestyle that will get you.
                         —Lee Trevino, on joining the Senior Tour

I guess I'm getting too old, but it took a long
time for them to catch up with me.
                         —Sam Snead, at age sixty-four,
                                   on young players

383

You know you're on the Senior Tour when your back goes out more than you do.

—Bob Bruce

Somebody is going to wake up one morning and realize the Senior Tour is not a bunch of over-the-hill guys.

—Hale Irwin

I'm getting so old, I don't even buy green bananas anymore.

—Chi-Chi Rodriguez

Everyone used to say to me, 'Glad you won the tournament' . . . and now they say, 'Glad you made the cut.'

—Arnold Palmer

That's the easiest 69 I ever made.

—Walter Hagen, on turning sixty-nine

One of the nice things about the Senior Tour is that we can take a cart and cooler. If your game is not going well, you can always have a picnic.

—Lee Trevino

Some of these Legends of Golf have been around golf for a long time. When they talk about having a good grip, they're talking about their dentures.

—Bob Hope

I play by memory. If somebody tells me to hit the ball 150 yards, I hit it 150 yards.

—Sam Snead, on his poor vision

I don't want to be eulogized until I'm dead.

—Ben Hogan, turning down an invitation to be the honoree at Jack Nicklaus's memorial tournament

The older I get the better I used to be!

—Lee Trevino

I'm just tired. It has been a long grind. There were days when I thought I would scream if I had to go to the course. It was week-in, week-out for years. I tried to give my best to golf. Now I want to realize a dream . . .

—Byron Nelson

His nerve, his memory, and I can't remember the third thing.

—Lee Trevino, on the three things an aging golfer loses

People have always said, 'Jack, I wish I could play like you.' Well, now they can.

   —Jack Nicklaus, at age fifty-four

That's life. The older you get, the tougher it is to score.

   —Bob Hope

You know you're getting old when all the names in your black book have 'M.D.' after them.

   —Arnold Palmer

When you die, what you take with you is what you leave behind. If you don't share, no matter how much you have you will always be poor.

—Chi-Chi Rodriguez

There aren't many fifty-year-olds beating twenty-year-olds. I was born at night, but it wasn't last night.

—Lee Trevino, on being in the Masters hunt at the age of fifty

When you get this old, you wake up with a different pain each day. Besides, it's a grind trying to beat sixty-year-old kids out there.

—Sam Snead

It's a lot nicer looking down on the grass instead of looking up at it.
—Arnold Palmer, on playing his 43rd Masters

Once a guy gets past fifty, if he misses one day of playing, he goes back two.
—Sam Snead

The older you get, the stronger the wind gets—and it's always in your face.
—Jack Nicklaus

Why the hell would people love that? I don't know. So Lee Trevino can make some more millions. It's a farce.
—John McEnroe, on the Senior Tour

I'm going to die in a tournament on the golf course. They'll just throw me in a bunker and build it up a little bit.

—Lee Trevino

I'll shoot my age if I have to live to be 105.

—Bob Hope

Guys, when you get to seventy, you're allowed a mulligan.

—Gary Player

The road's getting shorter and narrower, but I'll play wherever pigeons land.

—Sam Snead, at age eighty-one, 1994

I'm not a real smart guy. But I've got enough
brains to realize that when I'm sixty years old
and play a sport, that it's downhill.

—Lee Trevino

Don't ever get old.

—Ben Hogan, when he withdrew
from the Houston Open because
of pain and fatigue, 1971

I've been playing the game so long that my
handicap is in Roman numerals.

—Bob Hope

Because once you sit on your ass, you die. I've
got to keep active. It's what keeps me young,
keeps me going to the gymnasium, setting
goals for myself in business and in life. It's
all part of my life—traveling, meeting people.
That's the big thing. I love people.
　　　　　—Gary Player, on why he continues
　　　　　　　　to play golf competitively

I'm never satisfied. Trouble is, I want to play
like me—and I can't play like me anymore.
　　　　　　　　—Jack Nicklaus, at fifty